ART
for the ELEMENTARY EDUCATOR

A Teacher's Workbook for
Writing Integrated Lessons

Kendall Hunt
publishing company

Jeanette
WACHTMAN
Kennesaw State University

Cover image © Shutterstock, Inc.

www.kendallhunt.com
Send all inquiries to:
4050 Westmark Drive
Dubuque, IA 52004-1840

Copyright © 2016 by Kendall Hunt Publishing Company

ISBN 978-1-4652-8836-3

Printed in the United States of America

DEDICATED TO ALL EDUCATORS

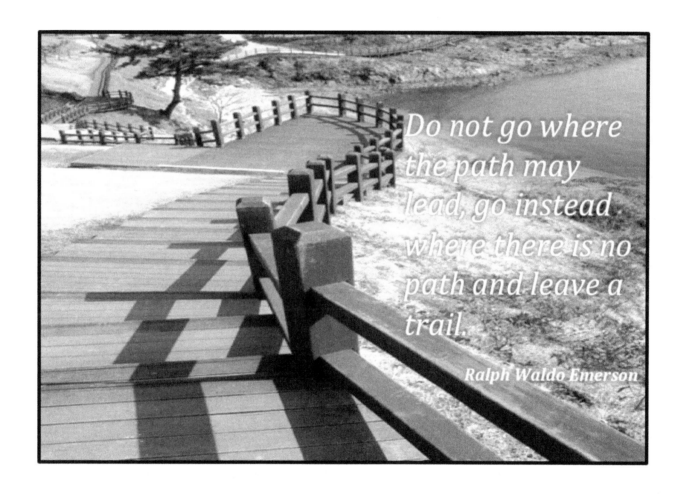

Do not go where the path may lead, go instead where there is no path and leave a trail.

Ralph Waldo Emerson

INTRODUCTION

A world without color! Shades of gray are everywhere. Going through life, existing in a gray bubble. It's not an exciting thought. I fashioned this dull and dreary image, so we may reflect and welcome how our daily lives and environments are enriched by color.

As educators we 'color' and enhance the lives of our students in the form of creativity, imagination, energy, emotion, vitality, and the excitement of learning. We embrace our students with this 'color' by how we interact and what we teach. We teach Science, so students can discover new planets. A new invention is the outcome of acquired Math skills. Social Studies classes expose world cultures inspiring one to travel and experience other societies. An achievement for a Language Arts student is writing a successful mystery novel. The Arts—Music, Theater, Dance, and Visual Arts—also inspire creative and imaginative endeavors. Many a student dreams of receiving a standing ovation for a theatrical performance, playing their favorite instrument in an orchestra, or being described as the next Martha Graham. Student artists begin first with scribbles on their family's wall.

Then, they evolve creatively through painting or sculpting of their innermost emotions, and successfully and proudly display the work for their audience.

Visual Arts include traditional fine arts, such as drawing, painting, printmaking, photography, and sculpture. The media arts include film, graphic communications, animation, and emerging technologies. Other areas include architecture, industrial art, folk art, and works of art such as ceramics, fibers, jewelry, wood, paper, and other materials (as defined by the National Art Education Association, Revised July 2014).

Previously, the educational arena has taught subjects in a departmentalized manner—Science for the sake of Science, Math for the sake of Math, etc. However, contemporary examination on how humans learn, based on neuroscience research, is providing an enormous amount of information on brain function. With this knowledge, it is important for educators to realize how this research influences our teaching strategies as we engage the student in a learning environment.

According to Jensen (2001), based on what we know about the brain and learning, the arts can enhance cognition, emotional expression, perception, cultural awareness, and aesthetics, which all can play a significant role in the learning process and should be thoroughly integrated into every subject.

Art educators, who have been overlooked for many years by mainstream education, have already been innately integrating classroom discipline concepts within their art lessons. Illustrations accompany a story, color theory explains the aspects of light, forms evolve into new structures, and ancient world images intensify the study of history.

This workbook is not the 'traditional' academic textbook. Within its pages, I have created a fictitious principal, teachers, reports, and stories in order to express a realistic representation from different applicable viewpoints in education. In addition, this workbook contains examples of hands-on, integrated lessons with artwork and pertinent knowledge for the educator to employ when teaching, thus creating an environment that is meaningful and supportive for student learning.

As I wrote this workbook, I employed a teaching strategy whereby the instructional content, what I want the reader to learn, was interwoven within an engaging storyline. The workbook's major topics include: Creativity, Art Styles, Aesthetics, Art Criticism, an Integrated Teaching Unit, Art History, Stages of Children's Art, a Thematic Cultural Program, and Lesson Plans using classroom subjects with students' artwork.

Throughout the book are "Art Pages," placed at the end of each lesson. These artistic pages contain geometric shapes, which can be used to display photos of your students' artwork. A majority of these art pages were made using various art techniques such as crayon resist, watercolor with salt applied to create patterns, and manipulation of photographs using Word docx. In addition, pages entitled "Teacher's Talent Project" encourage the teacher to dabble in art making and exploring his or her creativity.

This engaging narrative, with its imaginary stories and teachers, contains original rhymes used as a teaching tool. There is a story behind the making of these rhymes. Early in my career, I came across a teaching challenge. During art class, in a brand new school, students had difficulty paying attention and showed little interest in art making. There was a need to reevaluate my teaching approach at this school.

After research and attending workshops on how the brain learns, some new ideas surfaced. One strategy to engage the mind was to use rhymes and movement. I used this technique, writing original rhymes, to teach the Elements and Principles of Art. At first, students thought rhyming was weird, however they gradually began to enjoy moving and rhyming. Along the way, they impressed themselves by expressing what they learned in art. The second strategy was to enhance students' perception about the value of creating art. I accomplished this by inventing the "Art Store," which was supported by the PTA to sell students' artwork such as drawings and clay pins to parents, teachers, and the community. When a student received a check for $1.00 for selling his artwork, the words, " I'm an artist!" resounded in the hall. A change in attitude and learning occurred in the students. It is important, as an educator, to be flexible and to stay informed of new teaching ideas, no matter how out-of-the-box the strategies may be.

I have penned this workbook from the perspective of fictitious educators, an art teacher, and six classroom teachers from kindergarten through fifth grade. They share their lessons and art projects, along with some thoughts about their day's activities.

Meet the characters in this story:
- The kindergarten teacher is Mary. She is a new teacher, young and single, who always wanted to be a kindergarten teacher, loves the children, and is always smiling.
- Lewanda is a first-grade teacher who just came back from a trip to Europe and Africa. She likes to travel and share her experiences with her students. First grade is okay, but she wishes she was still teaching fourth grade.
- The second-grade teacher is Jerome. He has three daughters at home and his wife is also a teacher. He likes teaching second grade, and hopes to stay at this level for a few years.
- Esther teaches third grade, and is close to retirement from teaching. She loves third grade, and has devoted her life to her students. She wonders what she will do after retiring.
- The fourth-grade teacher is Tamara, and she was switched from first grade to fourth this year. She is a little nervous about teaching a new level and is pleased to find supportive teammates.
- Lynn is an experienced and gifted fifth-grade teacher. He is working on his masters degree and wants to become an administrator.
- Sharlene, the art teacher, has over 20 years of experience teaching art. She is well known in the art education field as an accomplished presenter at art

conferences on the creative teaching units she has designed and taught. In addition, she likes the opportunity to work with classroom teachers and provide art workshops for them. She also likes to paint, when she finds the time in her busy schedule. She travels to other countries during vacations with her husband, takes a lot of pictures, and uses them in her art lessons. Sharlene is excited about sharing art practices, and presenting art education concepts in workshops for the classroom teachers.

In the field of education, it is important not only to teach the academics, but also to provide for students the experience of creative activities. This workbook is an accumulation of over 35 years of teaching art and sharing the wonderful world of storytelling and imagination.

Jeanette Wachtman

ABOUT THE AUTHOR

Jeanette Wachtman is assistant professor of Art Education (PT) at Kennesaw State University in Kennesaw, Georgia. She began teaching in 1973 and throughout her career has taught students on all educational levels, including pre-kindergarten through to higher education. Throughout her teaching career, Wachtman has been active by presenting approximately fifty workshops and lectures at art and educational conferences, at international, national, and state venues. These presentations have focused on her a long-standing interest in sharing a thematic approach for designing cultural arts programs. Invited by the president of Seoul's Hanyang University, South Korea, examples of such programs were presented by Wachtman to art education Hanyang University students in 2010.

During her teaching career, as an art teacher in the public schools, Wachtman was the recipient of numerous awards and grants. She received the *Southeastern Elementary Art Educator Award* in 1999 from the National Art Education Association and *Georgia's Elementary Art Educator of the Year* in 1997-98, presented by Georgia's Art Education Association. While teaching at Kennesaw State University she was awarded grants that supported research, travel, and the presentation of original educational programs on the Peruvian, Korean, and Turkish cultures. Her current teaching interest includes the implementation of her course in an online format.

As a visual artist, Wachtman has received numerous awards in juried exhibitions. Her watercolor paintings, pottery, and photography have been exhibited in art galleries, one-woman, and national venues since 1977. As an author, her books on art programs exemplify innovative educational tools for teaching, self-published by her business RaJean & Company. Presently, she lives on five acres in the Georgia mountains with her four cats.

ACKNOWLEDGEMENTS

This workbook is the result of a collaborative effort with educators who are experts in their fields. I wish to acknowledge their contributions and express my gratitude for their support and determination in providing student artwork and releases for this workbook. The wonderful creative expressions in this workbook have been made possible through the contributions of student artists, including elementary through university levels. Because no book can be written without editorial help, a heartfelt thanks to Tamara Bolden, Sandra Bird, and Pipar West and their proficiency for the written word.

The following Art Educators contributed their valuable time and energy for this enterprise:

Mary Kaltreider, East Side Elementary, Cobb County, GA
Kathleen Frost, Lewis Elementary, Cobb County, GA
April Arnett, Ball Ground Elementary, Cherokee County, GA
Colleen Wachtman, Bascomb Carmel Pre-school, Cherokee County, GA
Mi Kormos, Fair Oaks Elementary, Cobb County, GA
Amy Brown, Vero Beach Elementary, Vero Beach, FL
Amelia Zschaber, Pine Mountain Middle, Cobb County, GA

In appreciation, I wish to recognize distinguished educators whose expertise in the field of Art Education led to scripted articles published throughout this workbook. Educators from Kennesaw State University, Kennesaw, GA include: Dr. Diana Gregory, Dr. Sandra Bird, Dr. April Munson, and Dr. Rick Garner.

Additional contributors include: Dr. Melody Milbrandt, Georgia State University, Atlanta, GA; Mary Partow, Art Specialist, Vero Beach High School, Vero Beach, FL; and Dr. Miwon Choe, Western Kentucky University, Bowling Green, KY.

CONTENTS

NOTES

NOTES

Day One: Monday

NOTES DURING LUNCH

I can't wait to share with other teachers my Language Arts writing lesson this morning! The kids loved the presentation. It is very important to provide an atmosphere to foster creative experiences for students in the classroom. So, my students went into outer space today, on an imaginary trip.

I converted my classroom to create the environment of outer space. I added posters of planets, a galaxy, meteorites, and constellations on the wall. I reviewed definitions: the Earth is in the Milky Way Galaxy; a number of constellation names are written on the board; the Earth's Sun is a star; and meteorites are large rocks that travel through space. The white board was used to present a 23-second YouTube video on a 3-D animation of a nebulae.

(Retrieved September 25, 2014 from https://www.youtube.com/watch?v=fl1SFN2pDfE#action=share.)

To heighten the feeling of traveling into space, I used a tape recording of a count-down and the sounds of a space ship blasting off. I wrote a script that described a dangerous space trip to a new planet, and after they landed on the planet, students were instructed to draw their experience. Upon returning to Earth, students wrote a story about their trip.

To start the lesson and the outer space adventure, I asked the students to close their eyes and place their heads down on the desk. I turned down the lights and read *Outer Space Story*.

OUTER SPACE STORY

You are an astronaut climbing into your space ship. This is a dangerous trip through space. You are the only one who volunteered for the trip because you are very brave. You press the button, the engines start to roar, and you hear the count-down (started the tape), 10...... 5, 4, 3, 2, 1, **Blast off**.

As you leave the planet Earth, there is darkness. The ship passes the Moon, Mars, and Jupiter. As you travel toward the constellation of Pegasus in the Milky Way, an alarm goes off, a warning of an incoming meteorite shower.

If meteorites hit the ship, the oxygen could be lost, and the mission could fail! Quickly you press the warp speed button and you travel faster-than-light through the universe's dark matter. As you approach the Andromeda Galaxy, you enter the coordinates for the planet KELT-1b. As the ship lands on the surface of the planet, hot gases damage part of the internal wing, which could cause the ship to become unstable on the return trip to Earth.

As you step out of the ship, the gravity is so strong it is difficult to raise your space boots to walk. As you look around, you are surprised by what you see. Strange colors and shapes fill the sky. There is an unusual landscape, and plants. In the distance someone or something is moving toward you.

FIGURE 1-1

ART FOR THE ELEMENTARY EDUCATOR

Essential Questions

How would you compare living in outer space to living on earth?
What conclusions can you draw from space travel?
Can you recall the names of the planets you passed on your 'trip'?

Outer Space Art Project

At this point in the story, students recorded what they "saw" by drawing and coloring a picture, and used the checklist as a resource (1-1, 1-2, 1-3).

Complete art steps 1 and 2 at an earlier time so papers can dry.

1. White tempera paint is splattered on 12" x 18" black construction paper for stars.
2. Paint the colors pink, blue, green, and yellow using watercolors, on 12" x18" white paper.
3. Draw and cut 5 different size circles for planets, on the watercolor paper. In each circle, make craters by drawing little circles and make shadows on each planet using black oil pastel.
4. To make the planet's surface, use the remaining watercolor paper and glue it to the bottom of the black construction paper.
5. Glue all planets on the black paper, draw images such as an astronaut, aliens, space ship, and any additional details using oil pastels.

FIGURE 1-2

After the students finished their art, I darkened the room, and had the students put their heads on their desks and close their eyes. I introduced the second part of the lesson: The Return Trip To Earth.

As you climb back into your space ship, lightning fills the sky, large balls of ice are crashing down, and you hear volcanoes erupting in the distance. You must leave right now! Waiting too long is dangerous. In your space ship, as the engines start, you accelerate to warp speed and make it safely into space. There is darkness. You navigate through space gases and meteorite clusters to Earth. In the distance you see the "blue marble" called Earth, and upon landing, you are congratulated on your outer space adventure with a medal of bravery.

LANGUAGE ARTS WRITING PROJECT:

Lights were turned on and students were introduced to the second part of this lesson, which was writing a creative narrative. I reviewed the criteria for the story and science words were spelled on the board. Students referenced the checklist for reminders. When students finished the assignment, they shared their art and story. Watching them talking and sharing their adventure was worth all the theatrics.

"One day I was on my space ship. I was running out of gas and I saw the planet Happy World. When I was stuck on the planet I met four creatures. They were always happy. Then I found some buildings. I found one that was off the ground. Then I was putting the Mexico flag on the ground. On that day I found one of the aliens on a shape ship and then I had to go home."

RS's Written Report

FIGURE 1-3

OUTER SPACE LESSON

The students reviewed Essential Questions placed on the bulletin board along with the lesson's rhyme for the students to learn. The teaching strategies such as incorporating rhymes, visualizations, and art producing within a lesson enhances learning by engaging the part of the brain that supports long-term memory (Tate, 2008).

OUTER SPACE RHYME

Outer space is the place to be
With comets, stars and galaxies.
Dark energy keeps the planets in line,
And lets the universe expand and shine.

Vocabulary

Geometric Shape has length and width.
Freeform Shape has undefined edges.
Color is seen when light hits an object.
Form is a three-dimensional shape.
Galaxy is made up of stars, planets, and gases.
Nebulae is made up of space dust.
Milky Way is a galaxy in which the Earth is found.
Meteorite is a rock in outer space.
Constellation is a group of stars in the sky that form a shape.
Astronaut is a person who travels in space.
Wet on Wet is a watercolor technique of putting paint on a wet surface.

Art Materials:

12" x 18" Black construction and white drawing paper, pencil, oil pastels, watercolor, brushes, glue, white tempera paint

Standards

Language Arts Standards:
- 4.L1.d Order adjectives within sentences according to conventional patterns.
- 4.L2 Demonstrate command of the conventions of Standard English capitalization, punctuation, and spelling when writing.

National Visual Arts Standards:
- Creating: Cr1 VA: 1.4a   Brainstorm multiple approaches to create art or design problem.
- Creating: Cr1 VA: Cr2.1.4a   Explore and invent art making techniques and approaches.

Objectives: The student will:

- Write a narrative describing an imaginary trip to outer space.
- Produce artwork that depicts an environment on an imaginary planet.

Steps To Present Lesson

- Set up environment in the room, present the story, explain art project, checklist and writing lesson to students. Exhibit the artwork.

OUTER SPACE ADVENTURE – CHECKLIST & ASSESSMENT

Astronaut: _____ Class_____ Grade ____

Include in your artwork: 5 pts. x 8 = 40 pts.
- ❏ Space ship
- ❏ You in your space suit
- ❏ Land characteristics
- ❏ Sky filled with colors, shapes, etc.
- ❏ Buildings - unusual shapes
- ❏ Plants
- ❏ Alien/Creature you met on planet
- ❏ Any action

Include Elements and Principle of Art: 4 pts. x 5 = 20 pts.
- ❏ Lines
- ❏ Geometric shapes
- ❏ Freeform shapes
- ❏ Colors
- ❏ Patterns

Steps for Art Work: 4 pts. x 5 = 20 pts.
- ❏ Paint papers
- ❏ Cut and glue shapes
- ❏ Draw items on planet using oil pastels
- ❏ Add details
- ❏ Fill up entire paper

Writing Story on *Outer Space Adventure*: 4 pts. x 5 = 20 pts.
- ❏ Interesting beginning & capitalization used correctly
- ❏ Name the planet
- ❏ Details added in story using adjectives
- ❏ Thoughts and feelings clearly expressed
- ❏ Final thoughts about the adventure

GRADE PTS._____

90-100 Exceeds Expectations = A
Rich in content full of thought and insight

80-89 Meets Criteria =B
Substantial information

70-79 Needs Further Development = C
Generally competent

0-69 Does Not Meet Expectations= D
Limited and Not Developed

Writing a Creative Narrative:

This narrative writing tells your adventure in Outer Space. Start with an interesting beginning to grab and keep the interest of the reader. Use many adjectives and details. Describe how you felt during the space trip, what you saw after landing, and **who** or **what** you met on the planet.

Creativity
Author: Diana Gregory

> *"Imagination is everything. It is the preview of life's coming attractions."*
>
> —Albert Einstein

For me, "going into space" in Tamara's fourth-grade classroom presents her students with an opportunity to explore and develop three important lifelong capabilities: to think creatively, to use their imaginations, and to learn while playing. The Partnership for 21st Century Learning (P21) recognizes creativity as an essential skill that all students need to succeed in college, career, and life. Creativity defined in literal terms is seen as thinking or problem solving that constructs new meaning, yet it is also the construction of personal meaning that is seen as self-expression and self-actualization (Runco, 2003). Looked at through this lens, as educators we need to remember that creativity is something that can be found in every child (Runco, 2008), indeed this view of "personal creativity" supports the notion of everyday creativity (Runco & Richards, 1998) or what Kaufman and Beghetto (2009) describe as "little-c" creativity in their Four C Model of Creativity.

Creativity can be found in every child. To help us understand creativity in this way, our focus will not be on objective performances and achievements, something that we would expect to find in Big-C creativity or eminence, but rather we will focus on the creative process itself and behaviors that support creativity like engagement with challenging tasks, involvement, and personal interest (Hennessey & Amabile, 2010). How can we as educators tap into students interests and find what is personally meaningful to them, then encourage them to work hard, take risks, and share with others even if it means facing rejection or worse? As educators, we have to find a way to strike the right balance between providing honest feedback that challenges students yet will support them to develop their creative competence (Beghetto & Kaufman, 2013).

> *"Creativity is putting your imagination to work."*
>
> —Ken Robinson

Eckhoff and Urbach (2008) ask a great question: "What if we viewed imaginative thought and creativity as fundamental to cognition?" (p. 179). In their research, they examine Vygotsky's (1930/2004) idea that imagination is a lifelong cognitive and affective undertaking that acts as a catalyst for all creative action.

They argue that integrating imaginative and creative thinking into the educational experience allows us to focus on a prospective view of education where problems are not yet known, rather than on a retrospective view of education where the focus is on mastering problems that are already known. This prospective view can be seen as "trans-disciplinary" knowledge that helps students move beyond looking for one "correct" solution, to an approach that integrates different solutions, viewpoints, or perspectives (Mishra, Koehler, & Henriksen, 2011).

With this prospective view of education in mind, Eckhoff and Urbach (2008) delineated Vygotsky's (1930/2004) four laws of imagination. First, imagination involves our daily activities and is a complex process that depends on personal experience (p.181), while the second law highlights one's ability to make use of social experiences of other people in imaginative activities allowing us to imagine outside of our experiential boundaries (p. 182). The third law highlights the link between imagination and emotion, and the fourth law examines how imagination becomes reality, as the building block of a new, external product, or an invention (p. 182).

Eckhoff and Urbach encourage educators to (1) design and implement the educational environment in such a way that children are encouraged to think imaginatively and learn to have faith and confidence in their imaginations (p. 182); (2) emphasize students' ability to engage in creative problem solving; and (3) empower children to develop imagination as an invaluable tool for understanding and contributing to their worlds (p. 185).

"Creativity requires the courage to let go of certainties."

—Erich Fromm

Marie Montessori and Jean Piaget noted that "play is the work of a child." In this view, play connects to Vygotsky's four laws of imagination. Child play, then learn as they play. Play is one of the "13 thinking tools of the world's most creative people" (Root-Bernstein & Root-Bernstein, 1999). Root-Bernstein & Root-Bernstein describe three types of play: practice play that contributes to the development of a skill set; symbolic play that involves meaning making; and game play that involves rule making that transforms play into a purposeful activity. While play may be seen as "just for fun," deep play is viewed as transformational (Mishra, Koehler, & Henriksen, 2015).

Deep play is characterized by its open endedness, a feature that contributes to its potential to inspire creative, boundary-extending ideas (p. 5). When Tamara arranged her classroom with the essential elements to go into space, she set the stage for her students to launch their imaginations giving them the opportunity to play, discover, form opinions, create, and finally to communicate their ideas to their peers. Creative thinking, problem solving, communication, and analytical skills are 21st-century skills of equal importance to academic and technical skills. They are lifelong skills that will serve the children into adulthood allowing them to pull together the pieces of their world while promoting social and emotional development. Tamara is supporting a prospective view of education by creating a nurturing environment that stresses the value of imaginative thought and a belief in possibilities. At heart she is supporting the natural talents of children while teaching them how to direct and control their creative tendencies (Runco, 2008). Finally and most significantly, Tamara is modeling what it means to be creative by demonstrating that imagination and play are valuable tools or habits of mind that are essential to express insights and to communicate ideas to others, thus reinforcing that old adage, children learn from what we do, not what we say.

Diana Gregory is Associate Professor and Chair of Special Education at Kennesaw State University. She earned an M.E. in Interrelated Special Education from North Georgia State University and a Ph.D. in Art Education from Florida State University. The field of creativity is a specialty of Dr. Gregory, who is sharing aspects of this topic based on her research.

CREATIVITY: A TRANSFORMATION ART ACTIVITY

Students using a Sharpie draw details to the shape to transform it into a recognizable or imaginary image. Instruct students to draw what objects are below and behind the transformed shape. Emphasize what is happening in the picture and adding details.

Day Two: Tuesday

MARY'S CLASSROOM
KINDERGARTEN

MORNING NOTES, RIGHT BEFORE THE BELL

Traffic this morning to school was awful along with the weather it was drizzly and the sky was grey. Some of the students are coughing. I'm glad I have a Par-a-pro to help me in the classroom. I check my email every day and noticed a priority message from the principal, addressed to all teachers related to lesson writing.

TO: CLASSROOM FACULTY

"In order to enhance student learning and improve scores, lessons will be written to include an interdisciplinary methodology. So, within a lesson plan include an objective, content, and assessment for an additional discipline. This approach provides our students a more meaningful learning experience because it eliminates a fragmented approach to teaching. Please prepare an integrated lesson, teach the lesson, observe students' reactions, and e-mail a brief report by next Friday. I am sure everyone is excited about enhancing our students' learning. A.L., Principal "

AFTER SCHOOL

I decided to write a lesson integrating math and art entitled "Super Geometric Robot." The lesson will be presented to the students tomorrow during math time. I was influenced to write this lesson after reading an article by Heidi Hayes Jacobs (2004) on intergraded learning. She stresses the importance to incorporate more than one discipline in a lesson using a central theme or topic. This approach enables students to begin to grasp connections among disciplines.

SUPER GEOMETRIC ROBOT LESSON

Essential Questions: Why do we learn math? Can you recall the names of geometric shapes? Can you describe how some geometric shapes are alike?

The questions are placed on the bulletin board along with the geometric rhyme for students to learn. The introduction of a mnemonic aid, words, and movement will help students remember the word geometric and the shapes.

Movement

- Students stand up and on each syllable when they say "Ge-o-met-ric" students click their fingers.
- When saying "Cha, Cha, Cha" students move their hips back and forth.
- When saying "Pssssss" one finger touches a hip.

Introducing The Lesson

The artwork entitled Pre-Bell-Man (2-1) by Nam June Paik is introduced to the students. The sculpture is composed of televisions and it appears that a figure is sitting on a horse. Students are told a story about the artist.

GEOMETRIC RHYME

Ge-o-met-ric,
Ge-o-met-ric,
Ge-o-met-ric
Cha, Cha, Cha
Pssssssssss

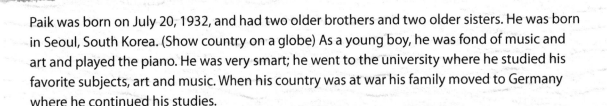

Paik was born on July 20, 1932, and had two older brothers and two older sisters. He was born in Seoul, South Korea. (Show country on a globe) As a young boy, he was fond of music and art and played the piano. He was very smart; he went to the university where he studied his favorite subjects, art and music. When his country was at war his family moved to Germany where he continued his studies.

His love of music inspired him to become an artist using music and electronic items such as TVs, radios, lights, and any object that plugged into the wall. His art is called Electronic Art. His artwork was very different from anybody else's. Paik was very creative and had many exhibitions, that is when people visit an art gallery and view your artwork. He was the very first artist who experimented with electronic media and is called the Father of Video Art. He helped people to see the world around them in a very different way.

As students view Paik's art they respond to the following questions:

- *What do you see in the picture?*
- *What did the artist use to make this sculpture?*
- *Can you make up a story about the person on the horse?*
- *Why do you think the person is on the horse?*
- *Where is the person going?*

The discussion continues:

- Is the horse and the figure flat or thick?
- Is a sculpture flat or can you see all around it?
- What kind of shapes do you see in the artwork?
- What colors are used the most?
- Are there any places that look bumpy, or look smooth?
- Do you like the artwork?
- What would you change in this artwork, if you were the artist?

FIGURE 2-1

Pre-Bell Man by Nam June Paik

MATH AND ART LESSON
Objectives: The student will:

- Identify geometric shapes: circle, square, triangle, and rectangle.
- Produce artwork that uses geometric shapes.

Standards

National Math Standards: MCCK:
- Correctly name shapes regardless of the orientations or overall size.

National Visual Arts Standards:
- Creating: VA Cr2.1Ka   Through experimentation build skills in various approaches to art making.

Vocabulary

Line is a dot moving in space.

Geometric Shape has length and width with clear edges (circle, square, triangle,. etc.).

Pattern is created by the repetition of lines, shapes, and colors.

Sculpture is a three-dimensional form having length, width, and thickness.

Art Materials:

12" x 18" black construction paper, pieces of cardboard, tray of white tempera paint, circular tools, oil pastels

ROBOT ART PROJECT

1. Each student views a demonstration by the teacher on how to make squares and rectangles by using a piece of cardboard.
    The edge of cardboard is dipping into a tray of white tempera paint and pressed onto the black paper, making edges (lines) to form geometric shapes. The circle-making tool is used to make details.
2. The teacher instructs the students that each robot must be built using rectangles, circles, and squares

FIGURE 2-2

ART FOR THE ELEMENTARY EDUCATOR

to make a head, body, arms, legs and include on the face the eyes, nose, and mouth.

Art Project Setup

Center 1 contains the trays of white paint. Students one-by-one take their black paper to the center. Under par-a-pro supervision students create their geometric shapes.

Center 2 contains a film container (or any tool that can make small circles) that is dipped in white paint and pressed on black paper to make circles and details. Let the paint dry.

Center 3 has boxes of oil pastels. A review on how to color is demonstrated by the teacher. While holding the oil pastel stick, the teacher shows the students how to move their wrist back-and-forth and color slowly in the same direction. After the paint on the paper has dried, the students color in the shapes.

Assessment

1. Complete art project using geometric shapes (circles, squares, rectangles) and fill in the checklist.
2. Teacher's observation: students identify the geometric shapes found in their artwork and in the classroom.

FIGURE 2-3

CHECKLIST FOR ART PROJECT

NAME _____

Make a "X" if your robot has the following:
- ❏ Squares
- ❏ Rectangles
- ❏ Circles
- ❏ Body
- ❏ Head
- ❏ Arms
- ❏ Legs
- ❏ Eyes
- ❏ Mouth
- ❏ Nose

Update: Report to the Principal

My lesson objective was the identification of geometric shapes, and artwork that incorporated geometric shapes. Students were introduced to a famous artist and his work as motivation. Based upon my observations, students were eager to tell their story about the robot on the horse. They were very animated when we performed our rhyme and movement.

The students were very careful when making their geometric shapes using the white paint. When it was time to color, they worked slowly and intensely. Robots were given names and students thought it was "cool" to have made a robot with superpowers.

After the art project was completed, students displayed their knowledge of geometric shapes by using the checklist and identifying the shapes as they moved throughout the room. In my opinion, art integration and using these teaching strategies motivated my students and their learning.

FIGURE 2-4

Teacher's Design of a Super Geometric Robot
Steps: draw with pencil, trace with ultrafine Sharpie, then color in using crayons and add two superpowers by drawing those characteristics on your robot.

Day Three: Wednesday

JEROME'S CLASSROOM
SECOND GRADE

LUNCHTIME NOTES

The morning lessons went well. I called my wife to pick up the kids after school, because we have Sharlene's art workshop after school. In fact, we will have art workshops for the next three Wednesdays. The principal is supporting an integrated approach for teaching students, and encouraging art activities to be incorporated within classroom lessons. Sharlene is excited about sharing Art Education concepts, art techniques, and ideas with the teachers.

AFTER SCHOOL: ART WORKSHOP IN THE MEDIA CENTER

Everyone has arrived and thank goodness there are some cookies and drinks.

INTRODUCTION BY SHARLENE:

Today's topic is information on the **Role and Importance of Art Education**. The article I am handing out today was written by a well-known author and art educator. After reading the article, any questions will be discussed. At the end of the workshop, I will pass out a resource entitled, **Guideline for Art & Classroom Lessons**. Its purpose is to help you select an art image and technique that can be integrated within your lesson plans.

HANDOUT ARTICLE ON ART EDUCATION

Role and Importance of Art Education
Author: Melody Milbrandt

The field of art education, like education in general, has traditionally been responsive to the contextual needs of society in the preparation of responsible capable citizens. Initially rising from a need for developing drawing skills in colonial America, over the past 50 years or so there have been a variety of purposes emphasized within the field of art education.

After World War II in the late 1940s and 1950s, Viktor Lowenfeld championed children's self-expression as the most fundamental purpose of art education, and defined developmental stages in children's drawings that influenced the scope and sequence of art instruction for decades. During the mid to late 1950s and 1960s, creativity emerged as an educational need during the U.S.–Russia space race. During the same time period, discussions about Abstract Expressionist artwork directed attention to the formal qualities of art, so teaching elements and principles of design became more central to art education curriculum. Throughout the 1970s the multicultural art education movement expanded the canon of formal qualities to include non-Western and women artists in the art curriculum. Discipline Based Art Education (DBAE) with focus on the four content areas of art history, art criticism, aesthetics, and studio art was a response to the reductivist attitudes of the 1980s Back to Basics educational movement. While initial DBAE models appeared to some as elitist, due to the focus on Western art, the structure of the four areas of study (art history, art criticism, aesthetics, and studio) had a major impact on the field.

In a DBAE curriculum, students who did not perceive themselves as strong studio artists could still excel in other aspects of the lesson. The purposes of art education refocused on the importance of all students engaging in a quality art education as a consumer, as well as a producer, of art. This trend toward a comprehensive art curriculum was further extended during the 1990s, with a focus on visual culture and the power of images in advertising and daily life. Since the turn of the century, technology has also played an increasingly important role in art education curricular developments.

The demand for computer animation and web design has redefined technology as a tool for artistic expression, and expanded the need for using such tools in the art classroom. In the current educational environment, with the emphasis on student growth accountability and the Common Core curriculum, a student-centered art education curriculum has emerged that supports student learning in a variety of ways.

The new Arts Core Standards emphasize key art understandings that guide lifelong learning in the arts, but allow teachers to construct lessons that best meet the needs of students in their classroom. Developing connections across content areas places learning in the arts within a school context to support learning in other disciplines, but also creates more depth in the meaning students bring to their artwork. There are many important reasons that all children should have equal access to a quality comprehensive arts education. In the complex demanding world of contemporary education, art education accomplishes multiple purposes simultaneously.

Art educators establish priorities in their teaching that encompass standards and outcomes set by the state and district, as well as meet the developmental and social needs of individual students, so art teaching can be highly contextual with lessons developed to meet the needs of students in specific schools and communities. However, I believe that rigorous learning in the visual arts generally engage students in rich experiences that support important educational goals and student developmental needs by (1) nurturing creative thinking, innovation, and problem solving; (2) supporting students' communication and expression; (3) building connections across disciplines; and (4) empowering students to engage with their community and society.

Art Education Fosters Creativity, Innovative Thinking, and Problem Solving

The need for creative, innovative designers and thinkers is a 21st-century global need, with the goal of creativity appearing in many international art curricula. In 2003, the Ministry of Education in Taiwan issued a white paper and a series of projects aimed at making Taiwan a "Republic of Creativity" where creativity is indispensable to life and creative pursuits are supported. Creativity is viewed as an asset for success and a goal for lifelong learning in Taiwan. Authors in the popular American press, such as economist Richard Florida (2005), have pointed out the importance of creativity for global economic growth. Others, like Daniel Pink (2006), see an increasing demand for creative thinking in all aspects of successful business life.

The United Nations Educational, Social and Cultural Organization (UNESCO) website suggests that worldwide support for creative industries is needed in developing countries to address and solve community problems (UNESCO, 2013). The Root-Bernsteins (1999) advocate that science educators teach students to approach problems more like artists, and Maeda (2013), with others, promotes the addition of Art to the Science, Technology, Engineering, Math (STEM) programs, making the acronym STEAM.

Flexibility in thinking is critical to the development of creativity and problem solving. Involvement in the arts teaches students to look at problems from a variety of viewpoints, shift their thinking, and explore ideas constructively. Students engaged in the arts not only learn how to find solutions to problems, but develop curiosity and perseverance to continually seek new problems to solve.

The Visual Arts Allow Students to Communicate a Variety of Messages, Develop Their Imaginations, and Express Themselves

The arts provide the tools for students to express feelings and ideas essential to the construction of personal identity and voice. The visual arts provide unique opportunities for expression of symbolic meaning that conveys more than verbal literal language. The arts help students form questions, explore their ideas, and engage in making and sharing meaning in productive ways. Constructing mental images is developmentally critical to young students learning to read and comprehend meaning. Images support students' understanding of text and enrich children's abilities to envision and construct worlds that can reflect and also reach beyond their limited experience with the world.

Creating visual arts provides students with opportunities to develop their fine motor skills in nonthreatening ways that can demonstrate the benefits of hard work, patience, and pride in project completion. Art education may offer young students ways to express a personal viewpoint, while developing understanding and skills of sequencing processes or exploring new materials. Finally, the visual arts give concrete form to abstract ideas and concepts essential for students' comprehension and understanding.

Engagement in the Arts Often Encourages Students to Build Connections Across Disciplines Through the Cultivation of Imagination

While engagement in the arts has not been empirically proven as a means to improve academic learning, research suggests that one of the most important key benefits of involvement in art education is the development of students' capacity for making connections across disciplines within school, and making connections from the art class to everyday experiences and events outside of school (Flanagan, 2009).

Through connection-making experiences, students are able to authentically construct knowledge and see its application and relationship to their world. While experiences in the arts may not necessarily improve academic achievement, there is research to show a relationship between involvement in the arts and a variety of achievements. Young people who participate in the arts are:

- Four times more likely to be recognized for academic achievement
- Three times more likely to be elected to class office within their schools
- Four times more likely to participate in a math and science fair
- Three times more likely to win an award for school attendance
- Four times more likely to participate in youth groups
- Twice as likely to read for pleasure compared with their non-art student peers (Flanagan, 2009)

One reason that students involved in the arts do better academically is their increases in attendance and graduation rates. A 2008 study by a non-profit organization found that the arts can play an important role in improving academic performance. In a national sample of 25,000 students, those students with high levels of arts-learning experiences earned higher grades and scored better on standardized tests than those with little or no involvement in the arts regardless of socioeconomic status. Learning through the arts also appears to have significant effects on learning in other disciplines, with students consistently involved in theater and music showing higher levels of success in math and reading (Catterall, Dumais, & Hampden-Thompson, 2012).

The Visual Arts Empower Students to Engage with Their Community and Society

There is evidence to suggest that students who are economically disadvantaged but have high levels of arts engagement and arts education show more positive outcomes in a variety of ways. These range from greater academic achievement to more positive civic involvement, and economic prosperity, than their low-arts-engaged peers (Catterall et al., 2012). In middle school, high school, and beyond, students tend to fare better on a host of academic and civic behavioral measures than do at-risk youth, who lack a deep arts background. To varying degrees, those outcomes extend to school grades, test scores, honor society membership, high school graduation, college enrollment and achievement, volunteering, and engagement in school or local politics.

At-risk teenagers or young adults with a history of intensive arts experiences show achievement levels closer to, and in some cases exceeding, the levels shown by the general population students. These findings suggest that in-school or extracurricular programs offering deep arts involvement may help to narrow the gap in achievement levels among youth of high versus low social-economic status. Youth from socially and economically advantaged backgrounds may also find access to greater civic and social participation via deep arts involvement

(Catterall et al., 2012). Sustained experiences in the arts form an educational portal, which can transform all students' lives and future.

The arts can also empower students to understand and affect their role in the community and society. Arts experiences can motivate individuals to become interdependent members of a global community. Exposure to multiple cultural perspectives through art challenges students to broaden their understanding of themselves and their world in relation to others, and offers numerous opportunities to empathize with others. This empowerment extends to encouraging students to find and value their voice, vital to the construction of identity, and develop relationships with others in the classroom and community. Finally, engagement in the arts can bring joy to all students as they explore and respond to their visual world.

This article was written by Dr. Melody Milbrandt, Associate Professor, Georgia State University, Atlanta, GA. She is well known in the scholastic field of Art Education as a writer, educator, and a presenter at many national and international conferences. Among her numerous writings, Milbrandt's current work includes the book, Art for Life, co-authored with Tom Anderson.

GUIDELINE FOR DEVELOPING AN INTEGRATED LESSON

Scenario: A new kindergarten teacher wants to integrate an art project in the science lesson, but is not sure where to start. Questions surface such as, *How do I go about deciding on an art project? What image should I use? What art materials and techniques are the best to use?*

The following themes are included in classroom disciplines:
- Language Arts Themes: *Narratives, Storytelling, Sequencing, Poetry, Grammar, Creative Writing, Literature, Folktales*
- Math Themes: *Geometry, Patterns, Graphs & Charts, Money, Add & Subtract, Multiply & Divide, Measuring, Fractions, Symmetry, 2-D, 3-D, Time*
- **Science** Themes: **_Earth Science_**, *Outer Space, Weather, Life Cycles, Fossils, Dinosaurs, Flowers, Animals,* **_Insects_**, *Technology, Human Body, Habitats, Wild Life, Life in Ocean, Cells,* **_Butterfly_**
- Social Studies Themes: *Famous Figures, Occupations, History, Diversity, Geography, Biography, Culture*

Following the steps in this guideline example can satisfy these questions.

Select:

1. Classroom discipline
2. Subject to be studied
3. Subject's image connected to focus of study
4. Art technique and materials
5. Introduce art language

Example:

1. Science is the classroom discipline. _
2. Earth science is the subject of the lesson.
3. The kindergarten activity is to identify the cycle of a butterfly.
4. The art project for this level is to make the shape of the butterfly by folding paper, drawing lines, and using scissors to cut on the lines. Crayons are used to color in the shapes (3-1, 3-2).
5. Art Language: symmetrical balance, curved and straight lines, warm and cool colors

SECTION 4 ART TECHNIQUES AND MATERIALS

The following art examples represent only a few of the numerous art techniques for the creative process.

Make a symmetrical shape: Fold the paper in half, place half of the shape on the fold, then cut, then open.

FIGURE 3-1

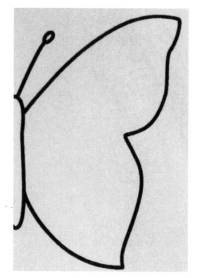

FIGURE 3-2   *Crayons*

FIGURE 3-3   *Oil Pastels (white pastel can be used to blend color as seen on right side)*

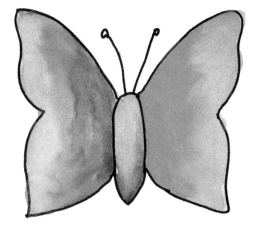

FIGURE 3-4   *Watercolor (water can be lightly placed on paper before watercolor to help move color)*

FIGURE 3-5   *Colored Markers (for large areas to color in, use the side of large marker)*

FIGURE 3-6   *Value – Pencil Repeat a line 3 or 5 times.*

FIGURE 3-7   *Line Designing. Value is determined by pressure on the side of a pencil's point, then smudge with tissue.*

ART FOR THE ELEMENTARY EDUCATOR

Project Collages:

FIGURE 3-8

Colored Tissue Collage (dilute white glue with water, cover paper and apply tissue)

FIGURE 3-9

Paper Collage (draw shapes, cut and glue)

When making a collage, a variety of materials can be used, such as images or text from magazines and newspapers, ribbons, paint, colored or handmade papers, and found objects that are glued to a surface.

PRINTING PROJECT
Styrofoam Plate with Design

 FIGURE 3-10   *Styrofoam Plate with Design*

FIGURE 3-11   *Colored with Markers*

FIGURE 3-12   *Print Pulling Print #1*

FIGURE 3-13   *Texture Rubbings*

PRINTING USING COLORED MARKERS:

On Styrofoam (plate) (3-10) lightly draw the design with pencil. Prepare the surface for printing: (1) Trace the drawing by pressing down on the lines with a pencil; make sure the groove is deep and wide. (2) Color the design with markers using a variety of bright colors.

On white paper, use a damp sponge and moisten the paper. Place moist paper **on top of the design** and gently press down and rub with thumb. Pull print #1, then using the same colored markers, color the plate again, wet paper and print #2. This process allows the artist to make multiple prints of the same image.

TEXTURE RUBBINGS:

Using the **side of a crayon**, place paper on top of a textured surface and rub. A pattern will appear. Let students use two or three different colors in the same area. A popular and fun surface to use is the bottom of sneakers. After a paper is filled with colors and textures, have students draw shapes on the paper, cut, and then glue shapes on new paper to make a picture.

NOTES

PROJECT: WEAVING

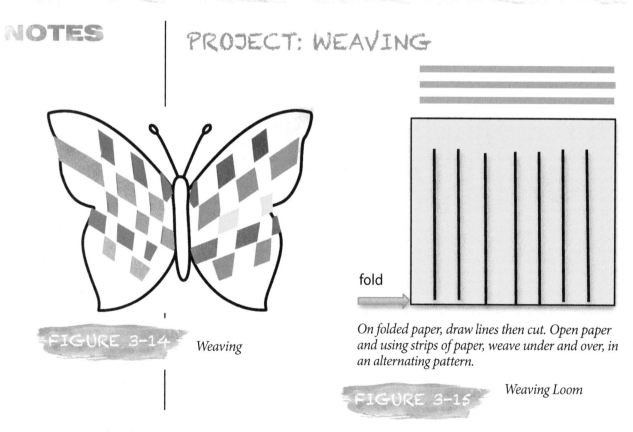

FIGURE 3-14 *Weaving*

On folded paper, draw lines then cut. Open paper and using strips of paper, weave under and over, in an alternating pattern.

FIGURE 3-15 *Weaving Loom*

FIGURE 3-16   *Resist Technique*
Brushed tempera black paint, diluted with water, over oil pastels

FIGURE 3-17   *Metal Relief*
Use 36-gauge aluminum tooling foil and place over a thick pad of newspapers. Design the surface with a pencil by pressing down hard. Black shoe polish can be brushed on top and then shined to create a contrast of silver and black.

ADDITIONAL IDEAS FOR ART PROJECTS

Three-dimensional art projects can be made from the following materials:

FIGURE 3-18   *Paper Sculpture*
Strips of paper are twisted, folded, curled, and glued to base.

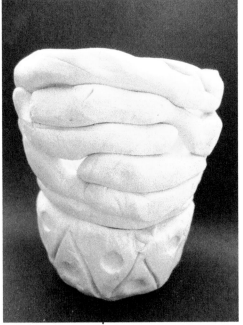

FIGURE 3-19   *Pottery Clay*
– bisque
Techniques
– pinch pot
and coil
making

ART FOR THE ELEMENTARY EDUCATOR

FIGURE 3-20

*Fired Pot, Painted
with Acrylics*

FIGURE 3-21

*Air-Dried Clay,
Bird with Feathers*

FIGURE 3-22

*Plastic Modeling
Clay
Set up an art cen-
ter with matching
color containers
with laminated
colored construc-
tion paper.*

SECTION 5. The following two worksheets illustrate the language of art; the **Elements and Principles of Art** used in the creative process of art making.

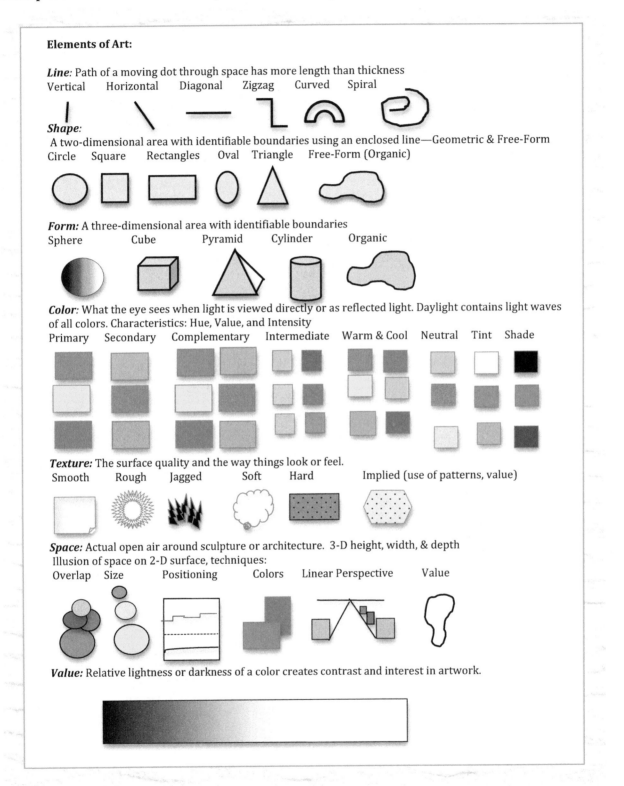

Elements of Art:

Line: Path of a moving dot through space has more length than thickness
Vertical   Horizontal   Diagonal   Zigzag   Curved   Spiral

Shape:
A two-dimensional area with identifiable boundaries using an enclosed line—Geometric & Free-Form
Circle   Square   Rectangles   Oval   Triangle   Free-Form (Organic)

Form: A three-dimensional area with identifiable boundaries
Sphere   Cube   Pyramid   Cylinder   Organic

Color: What the eye sees when light is viewed directly or as reflected light. Daylight contains light waves of all colors. Characteristics: Hue, Value, and Intensity
Primary   Secondary   Complementary   Intermediate   Warm & Cool   Neutral   Tint   Shade

Texture: The surface quality and the way things look or feel.
Smooth   Rough   Jagged   Soft   Hard   Implied (use of patterns, value)

Space: Actual open air around sculpture or architecture. 3-D height, width, & depth
Illusion of space on 2-D surface, techniques:
Overlap   Size   Positioning   Colors   Linear Perspective   Value

Value: Relative lightness or darkness of a color creates contrast and interest in artwork.

ART FOR THE ELEMENTARY EDUCATOR

Principles of Art:

Pattern: A repetition of lines, colors, shapes in artwork

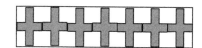

Balance:
The equilibrium of various elements in a work of art
Symmetrical: A mirror image—a visual balance

Asymmetrical: Two sides that do not correspond to one another in size, shape, and placement—a feeling balance

Radial Balance: Design initiates at the center and can be divided into two identical halves

Emphasis:
The center of interest—a focal point

Variety:
Differences in scale, surface, line, value, and shape that give interest and contrast to a composition

Visual Rhythm: Depends on the repetition of accented elements, usually shapes

Proportion: The pleasing relationship of all parts to each other and to the whole of the design

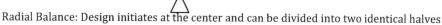

Unity: The sense of oneness, of things belonging together and making up a coherent whole

Day Four: Thursday

MORNING NOTES

Last night my daughters insisted I watch (again) their favorite movie, *Finding Nemo,* the Disney production about a fish. As I was watching, I came up with the idea that I could use a short section in the underwater scenes to introduce the science lesson on "Animal Life Cycles of Different Living Organisms." The bell just rang, the lesson will be written after school using Sharlene's "Art Project Guideline Worksheet" that she introduced at the art workshop Wednesday.

AFTER SCHOOL, DEVELOPING LESSON
Sharlene's Art Project Guideline Worksheet:

1. Classroom discipline: Science
2. Topic within this discipline:
    Life Science - Cycle of Life
3. Images connected with this topic:
    Fish, Shark, Octopus, Whale, Dolphin, Starfish, Turtle, Ocean Floor with Anemone, Shrimp, Lobster, Seaweed, Plants, Jellyfish (4-1), Seahorse (4-2), Coral (4-3)
4. Art Project: *Under the Sea*, using watercolor resist technique.

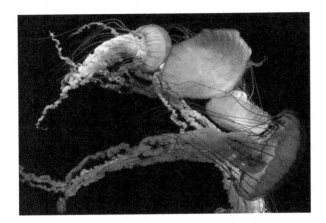

FIGURE 4-1

FIGURE 4-2

FIGURE 4-3

Photographs taken at Tennessee Aquarium, Chattanooga

UNDER THE SEA LESSON

Essential Questions

- What is so fascinating about underwater creatures?
- How would you describe the sequence of Nemo's lifecycle?
- How would you describe life at the bottom of the sea?

These essential questions are placed on the bulletin board along with the fish rhyme for students to learn.

NOTES

Introducing the Lesson

Students will be introduced to the movie *Finding Nemo* and as they view the movie ask them to consider these questions: *Where in the movie do you find stages of the fish life cycle? Can you name sea creatures and fish you see in the movie?*

The beginning section of the movie includes the hatching of Nemo. At this point, the movie is stopped and a discussion on the lifecycle of a fish is explained and discussed. The movie is re-started and periodically stopped to identify the types of sea creatures in the ocean. The students will see the complete movie during special times during the next few days.

Big fish and little fish, whales and sharks too,
All swimming slowly, through the ocean blue.
Big fish and little fish, crabs and starfish too,
Crawling on the sand, in the ocean blue.
Big fish and little fish, lots of creatures too,
What's your favorite in the ocean blue?

SCIENCE CONTENT TO KNOW: FISH LIFE CYCLE: EGGS: FERTILIZED EGGS DEVELOP INTO FISH.

Definitions

Fry: young fish ready to start eating on their own
Juvenile: developing from fry into reproductively mature
Adult: when fish are able to reproduce
Spawning: when female fish release eggs into the water

Objectives: The student will:

- Identify the life cycle of a fish.
- Recognize sea creatures.
- Produce artwork depicting life at the bottom of the sea.

Standards

National Science Standard:
- 2.L.1.1 Recognize animal life cycles.

National Visual Arts Standards:
- Responding: VA: Re7.1.2a: Perceive and describe the characteristics of one's natural world and constructed environment.
- Creating: VA: Cr2.1.2a: Experiment with various materials schools to explore personal interests in a work of art or design.

Vocabulary

Life Cycle is the continuous sequence of changes undergone by an organism from one primary form to the development of the same form again.
Fish Life Cycle involves fertilized eggs developing into fish.

Art Materials:

Video: *Finding Nemo*
White drawing paper 8" x 11"
Black marker, crayons
Watercolor wash
Visuals: Google images for fish and underwater sea creatures—download and print as examples

Art Language

Line is a dot moving in space.
Geometric Shape has length and width.
Freeform Shape has undefined edges.
Color is seen when light hits an object.
Texture refers to the feeling of a surface.
Space is foreground, middleground, and background.
Watercolor Resist is a wash (diluted tempera paint) that covers oil pastels or crayons.

FIGURE 4-4

NOTES

UNDER THE SEA ART PROJECT

1. Draw at the bottom of the paper the ocean floor, with plants, seaweed, and sea creatures that grow, crawl, and live (two or more images).
2. Draw different types of fish in the ocean using a pencil (four or more images).
3. Outline all shapes with a black marker.
4. Color in shapes with crayons, pressing down hard when coloring.
5. Using wash paint surface of artwork

FIGURE 4-5

FIGURE 4-6

After completing the artwork, the students will fill in the *Under the Sea* Science worksheet. Next, students will color in yes or no color in the *Under the Sea* Art checklist for the artwork.

Under the Sea Science Worksheet

Drawing a line connect the sea creature with its name.
Write the stages for the life cycle of a fish in the bottom section.

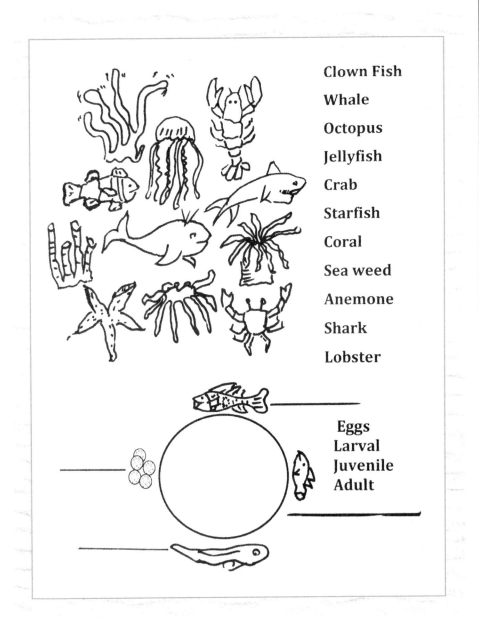

Clown Fish

Whale

Octopus

Jellyfish

Crab

Starfish

Coral

Sea weed

Anemone

Shark

Lobster

Eggs
Larval
Juvenile
Adult

UNDER THE SEA ART CHECKLIST

Directions: Students self-assess by coloring in YES or NO shapes based on drawings.

Items to be included in artwork	COLOR IN IF YES	COLOR IN IF NO
Ocean floor drawn		
Plants were drawn		
Seaweed was drawn		
2 or more bottom of the sea creatures were drawn		
4 or more fish drawn in the sea		
All shapes were outlined with black marker		
All shapes were colored in really hard		
Artwork was filled in with blue watercolor wash		

Day Five: Friday

LYNN'S CLASSROOM
FIFTH GRADE

LUNCHTIME NOTES

I received a new computer for my classroom this morning. The computer programs have been updated and I'm looking forward to discovering what new programs I can use in the classroom. The art teacher, Sharlene, and I are excited about working together to integrate a Social Studies lesson on Civil War with attention to photographer Matthew Brady; and a photographic art project that will concentrate on the environment.

Rationale

It is the 21st century and like it or not, our students are constantly using their phones to document the world around them, whether it be in the form of selfies or videos of their friends. There is hardly a student out there now who does not have access to a camera, yet there is surprisingly few resources for them to use the cameras more effectively. This lesson was designed with support from the art teacher in collaboration with the classroom teacher to embrace the wave of technology with a lesson taken from two different historical points of view.

Social Studies Lesson

Learning about the past, why is it important?
This is the lesson's essential question placed on the bulletin board.

PHOTOGRAPHY IN THE ELEMENTARY CLASSROOM – DOCUMENTING THE WORLD

National Social Studies Standards

- Nss-Ush.5-12.5 Era 5: Civil War and Reconstruction (1850-1877)
- Standard 2: The course and character of the Civil War and its effects on the American people.

Objectives: The student will:

- Interpret and write opinions based upon images in Civil War photographs.
- Demonstrate the interdisciplinary relationship of Social Studies, Science, Technology, Language Arts, and Visual Arts.

Matthew Brady documented the Civil War and has been called the father of photojournalism. His photographs included battlefields, camp life, and portraits of famous individuals such as Abraham Lincoln, U.S. Grant, Robert E. Lee, and General Sherman.

Research for the lesson:

The following sites provide images to use in the PowerPoint presentation.
- http://www.history.com/photos/civil-war-mathew-brady#
- http://www.civilwar.org/education/history/biographies/mathew-brady.html
- http://www.npg.si.edu/exh/brady/war/blee.htm
- http://www.npg.si.edu/exh/brady/gallery/57gal.html

Introduction of Civil War Images

Students viewed a powerful PowerPoint presentation of photographs of the Civil War, taken by Matthew Brady. Photos of Lincoln and Sherman flashed on the screen, along with a variety of images of camp life and group portraits. Included in the presentation are photographs from a Civil War battle of fallen soldiers. Discussion led to note taking as students began answering the following questions:

- What do you think civilians felt when they saw what happened on a battle-field for the first time?
- How did the war affect the lives of civilians?
- What do these photos show you about what life was like as a soldier?
- What do you believe their daily thoughts were about?
- Do you think the photographer was in danger?
- Would you like to be a photographer on a battlefield?

COMPONENTS:

- Social Studies
- History
- Language Arts

After the discussion, students used their notes to write their opinions based upon the questions.

Visual Arts Standards

Artistic Process: Relate artistic ideas and works with societal, cultural, and historical context to deepen understanding.
- *VA: Cn11.1.5a* Identify how art is used to inform or change beliefs, values, or behaviors of an individual or society.
- *VA: Cr1.1.5a* Combine ideas to generate an innovative idea for art making.

Objectives: The student will:

- Produce a photograph to document an aspect of their lives within their school environment.
- Write an essay describing their photograph and photographic experience.

Vocabulary

The *Civil War* is the war fought in the United States between northern (Union) and southern (Confederate) states from 1861 to 1865, in which the Confederacy sought to establish itself as a separate nation.

Documentation is the act or an instance of the supplying of documents or supporting references or records.

Technology is the branch of knowledge that deals with the creation and use of technical means and their interrelationship with life, society, and the environment, drawing upon such subjects as industrial arts, engineering, applied science, and pure science.

Elements and Principles of Art are the building blocks used to create a work of art.

Art Materials:

Civil War images
Digital camera(s)
Cellphone(s)
Photographic paper
Computer and ink
PowerPoint program

Assessments:

1. Social Studies History Lesson: Written opinions based upon images in Civil War photographs.
2. Visual Arts Project: Printed photograph, checklist completed, written essay describing the Principles of Arts in their photograph and thoughts about their photographic experience.

Background for Role of Photography

Part 1
Students reviewed Brady's Civil War photographs that initiated a discussion on the significance of this "new" technology, which documented the war in pictures.

Discussion began about the significant impact photography had on politics. People now could see actual pictures of their president and generals. Students discussed how this was different from painted portraits of the same people.

The focus of the discussion was to cement in the student's mind the first reason for photography: documentation. This would serve as the theme for art and history activities.

To further support this theme, famous photographs documenting key events in 20th-century history were presented: the famous "art" photograph by Dorothea Lange's anguished photo of a mother and children during the Great Depression; the raising of the flag at Iwo Jima; and *Dovima with Elephants*, a famous Richard Avedon photograph of a model in a Dior evening dress at the Cirque d'Hiver, August 1955. Students were surprised to learn this photo was a fashion shoot for Vogue.

COMPONENTS:

- Technology
- History

Introduction for Photography Project

Part 2

A PowerPoint presentation of Ansel Adam's photos of nature was presented to students. The photograph of *Sierra Mountains* initiated a discussion in terms of the Elements and Principles of Art: line, shape, form, texture, color, value, and space.

Students were asked to answer questions about value in the photographs: *What is the brightest part of the photo? What is the darkest part? How many shades of grey do you see? Is there a white section? Is there a black section?*

Students identified where lines repeated themselves to make patterns, where textures changed from smooth to rough, and where their eye was first drawn to when they first looked at the photo.

Each Principle of Art was written on the board: pattern, rhythm, movement, contrast, balance, emphasis, unity, and variety. Then, students in teams discussed where they found examples of these principles in Ansel's work.

COMPONENTS:

- Technology
- History
- Science
- Visual Arts

Art Project Criteria

Part 3

When documenting their life at school:

1. Photos will be in black and white and include a total of four images: one selfie (first photo) and three from the school's environment.
2. Photos will be taken from an unusual point of view, a very different angle than straight on.
3. The checklist will be used to identify the Principles of Art in their favorite photograph in an essay that describes the photograph and their thoughts about their photographing experience.

COMPONENTS:

- Technology
- Science
- Visual Arts

FIGURE 5-1

Procedure

Part 4

During art class, along with the classroom teacher, students walked around the school taking photographs, working in teams and sharing a cellphone or a digital camera. Students downloaded their images in the computer and selected their best shot to be printed onto an 8" X 10" image for display. After the students complete the checklist and essay writing, their work will be displayed.

FIGURE 5-2

Part 5

This format can be used to identify Principles of Art in photographs and enrich the essay writing about the photographic experience.

Principles of Art
Pattern
Rhythm
Movement
Contrast
Balance
Emphasis
Unity
Variety

CONCLUSION

Students have examined photographs recording historical events, applied the Elements and Principles of Art to an art project, composed and produced an interesting photograph, and benefited from participating in an interdisciplinary teaching unit incorporating Social Studies, Science, Technology, Language Arts, Visual Arts, and exhibiting their artwork.

Options-Extensions-Variations

Documenting the Civil War was an easy way to use this lesson to focus on social studies, but it can be altered with many themes in mind. This lesson can be applied for second graders who are studying plants. Instead of Ansel Adams, the artistic inspiration can be Edward Wetson, and his early black and white photographs of vegetables with a focus on macro photography and the rhythms and patterns found in plants and flowers. Identifying the parts of a flower photographed up close becomes the worksheet. This could be done for any scientific study where examples of the object of study can be closely observed.

FIGURE 5-3

FINAL THOUGHTS

As educators, we sometimes grapple with what is the most important aspect of our participation-based teaching methods. Is the process of creating more important than the final product, or is a successful product the ultimate goal as it creates excitement and enthusiasm for our program? While most educators shoot for a marriage of engaging process and engaging product, often one will trump the other. In this lesson, over the years, both the process and the product continue to balance.

Mary Adamski-Partow, an art teacher who has presented this lesson at the elementary level, designed this integrated history and art lesson. Presently, Partow teaches art at Vero Beach High School in Vero Beach, Florida. She has presented workshops and lectures at national, state, and local conferences on innovative educational programs that she designed and taught.

Art and the Aesthetics of Technology
Author: April Munson

Josh spends more than an hour each day engaged with the building of his digital self. Through multiple means of media, he changes fonts, uploads pictures, writes brief narratives, reflects, and finds friends with common interests. He utilizes a variety of symbols, signs, and emoticons to let the world know what he is thinking, how he is feeling, and where he is physically located. Not only does he actively engage with the construction of this digital representation of himself, he spends time, though not consciously, analyzing the impact of his choices. He knows that certain sets of symbols and imagery will construct a type of identity he wants to portray. He is focused on the aesthetic representation of himself in his technology. He is you. He is your student. He is everywhere.

The word "technology" stirs different feelings for each of us. Exhilarating. Frustrating. Fast. As educators, technology is in the language of the standards we work to achieve. The types of technology we use are often in direct correlation with what the schools offer in terms of physical materials, software, and access.

While theoretically the term technology *is defined as the product of human ability to create useful items or problem-solving mechanisms, depending on when you read this, you will have your own ideal of technology. More often than not, your students will have a different ideal of the purpose and defining of the term.*

Why technology and aesthetics?

As the use of technology has become deeply embedded within the everyday lives of Americans, certain issues involving technology begin to emerge. The particular issues in this section focus on aesthetics and technology in education and the everyday. Aesthetics, or "the study of the mind and emotions in relation to the sense of beauty," is a branch of the arts that is perhaps the most utilized in everyday life (aesthetics, n.d.). We have a definite sense of what looks "off" or out of place—be it in what we or others wear, the way a space is decorated or arranged, or an advertisement that beckons us to spend money. In the same vein, we have a deep sense of what is "put together" or has positive flow. These deep understandings of emotional and relational connections to experiences are near the very essence of aesthetics.

And, when we look closely, these understandings are also a critical component of quality use of technology. While the vast majority of our students will have spent a great deal of time, regardless of background, interacting with technology, few will have made the conscious connection between the idea of aesthetics and their technological world. This is a bridge waiting to be built by the teacher.

Helping our students translate their understanding of aesthetics into their world of technology will not only better prepare them to be successful in the world around them, but will support them as they become more critical in their thinking, and more aware of the hundreds of images they encounter daily. As teachers, developing a deeper understanding of aesthetic sensitivity in the use of technology enables us to be selective, intentional, and evaluative of the technology we incorporate. Our "eye" for technology changes; as our eye becomes more discerning, our breadth of knowledge of what is available and for what purpose in our teaching and learning is broadened. We continually strive to equip our students and ourselves with greater access to current technologies. We place in our students' hands and hold in our own hands the significant ability to manipulate and understand aesthetic statements.

And yet, without some sense of bridging the aesthetic and technology, we are left with users who don't have a sense of how to assess what they use or produce, and consumers who have yet to begin to understand how they, at any age, are targets of mass consumerism.

As teachers strive to build the bridge between aesthetics and technology, they are becoming champions of visual literacy and advocates for student discernment in a world saturated in images and the next new technology.

Visual literacy and an understanding of the aesthetics of technology are necessary for supporting the best and brightest citizens for our classrooms and our world.

The author, Dr. April Munson, is assistant professor in art education within the School of Art and Design at Kennesaw State University. Her research focuses on assessment of quality in the art classroom and invites students to offer suggestions both about the course content and her style of teaching. She is committed to being an active member in professional communities, so that her ideas of teaching, learning, research, and the field of art education continue to evolve.

A Flashback on Technology in the Classroom
Author: Jeanette Wachtman

In the olden days, referring to the 1970s, a teacher was elated to have technology in the classroom, such as an overhead projector. When using this equipment, the image or text was placed on the projector's light source, and it was then projected onto a white screen that was attached to the wall. The popular 35 mm single lens reflex cameras, such as Canon or Kodak, used print or slide film to record classroom activities. It took a week to retrieve the prints and negatives from the store that processed the film. Projecting pictures in sequence onto a white screen was achieved by using a slide projector. Educational slides could be purchased, or using slide film, teachers could create their own. Oh, yes, teachers and students used white chalk on blackboards.

The 21st-century classroom incorporates today's technology such as iPads, smartphones, and computers that connect the students to the world via the Internet, which prepares students for life, whether they're going to be using technology at home or at work. Over 30 educational-technology professionals have compiled a resource for hardware and software essentials for the classroom teacher at http://www.educationworld.com/a_tech/tech/ tech239.shtml (retrieved June 17, 2015).

Day Six: Monday

TAMARA'S CLASSROOM
FOURTH GRADE

MORNING BEFORE CLASS

Today is going to be a very busy day. Starting new lessons and then, on top of everything else, I received an email early this morning from the principal about a new approach for teaching one of our Social Studies units. The fourth-grade team, which includes Margaret, Leah, Colleen, and myself, will meet in the media center while the students are at specials, to begin collaboration on this teaching unit.

Tamara's Email Notes: During the first meeting today, the purpose is to review the following information for writing an integrated Social Studies unit on the Native American cultures, entitled "American Roots." The following are the topics that will be reviewed today:

- Part 1. Rationale for the introduction of cultural studies
- Part 2. Guidelines and themes for the teaching unit
- Part 3. Example of themes applied to the Incan culture
- Part 4. National Standards for Social Studies
- Part 5. Geographical regions of the Native American cultures

Part 1.

Rationale for the Introduction of Cultural Studies
Importance of Cultural Studies: The study of other cultures enables us to become aware of the diversity of others, their beliefs and material accomplishments wheth-

er it be monuments, art, literature, or philosophy. Exposure to other cultures will expand ways in which this world is perceived and how we respond to it. A multicultural approach in education and instruction encompasses the introduction of cultures, and is based upon building respect and fostering understanding.

Part 2.

Guidelines for the Teaching Unit
Guidelines: It is important to be specific when presenting information on a culture. For example, to address a specific group and its leaders, research beliefs and social systems, and present historical content accurately to avoid stereotypical thinking. It is important to be respectful and authentic when relating to ritual activities of a specific group. While teaching cultural traditions and customs of a specific culture, also introduce contemporary information. Finally, use sound historic references that focus on a specific group (Harnew, 1997).

Part 2 continued.

Themes for the Teaching Unit
Themes: Effective thematic instruction involves using a theme as the "conceptual glue" for learners, strengthening bonds to knowledge, and a way of understanding new concepts. Themes provide mental organizing schemes for students to approach new ideas (Caine & Caine, 1994) and have been shown to increase student achievement (Kovalik & Olsen, 1994).

Three Broad-Based Themes

People and the Environment, People in Society, *and* ***People and Their Beliefs*** are three broad-based themes. These three themes and subtopics were originally designed and taught in a cultural arts program by art teacher Jeanette Wachtman at the elementary level.

Developing broad-based themes is an essential element for a thematic program according to Kovalik's model, *Integrated Thematic Instruction (ITI)* published in 1989. Using these three themes when teaching Social Studies is applicable when teaching any culture—Peru, India, Japan, China, Australia, Turkey, or Africa.

Part 3. Example of Themes Applied to the Incan Culture

The following material is an example of the three themes applied when studying the Incan culture:

When studying the Incas of Pre-Columbian, Peru (1450–1532 CE), they constructed their buildings to match the surrounding landscape of mountains and tropical forests.

Well-cut stone blocks filled their cities as displayed at the famous Machu Picchu center (6-1). Mountainsides were transformed into terraces for farming corn, potatoes, and quinoa seeds. Nature provided soft wool (6-2) of the alpaca for weaving, and clay for pottery (6-3). This information reflects the theme *People and the Environment* that investigates what nature provides so people can live.

Students can explore environmental conditions and how natural materials are transformed to meet survival needs and to express creative imagery.

FIGURE 6-1

Machu Picchu, Peru

The theme *People in Society* explores the various roles the individual performs in society. Societal self-perception is manifested in shared political and social institutions, organizations, and activities. For example, the Incan king (6-4) had absolute power, ruling over rituals and festivals. Incan society was divided into two sections, nobles determined by blood history of the family, and citizens who were divided into groups: workers, artisans, and farmers (6-5) and public administrators.

Weaver from the Center for Traditional Textiles of Cusco, Peru

FIGURE 6-3

Killer Whale, Pottery Nazca Culture, 100 BCE – 800 CE Larco Museum, Lima, Peru

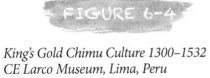

King's Gold Chimu Culture 1300–1532 CE Larco Museum, Lima, Peru

FIGURE 6-5

Peasant Workers on Taquile Island, Lake Titicaca

ART FOR THE ELEMENTARY EDUCATOR

Priests and priestesses were thought to be able to do the bidding of the gods, so they were highly honored and often part of the royal family. The government recorded its history and goods on quipus (6-6), a calculating tool of colored knotted cords.

FIGURE 6-6

Quipu, Talking Knots Inca Culture 1438–1533 CE Larco Museum, Lima, Peru

The theme *People and Their Beliefs* probes belief systems and how these beliefs manifested within a society. Accepted tenets are conveyed in myths, rituals, garments, movement, music, images, and architecture. For example, the polytheistic Incas' main god was Viracocha and his believers were known as the "Children of the Sun."

FIGURE 6-7

Burial Scene, Illustration Huaca Pucllana Museum, Lima, Peru

They worshiped gods of nature; the sun god, the god of thunder, moon, rainbows, mountain tops, stars and planets. They believed that the gods and their dead ancestors could communicate with them through shamans, dreams, omens, and other signs. The powerful priests, who could read the communication signs, directed major religious festivals that included games, songs, dancing, music with drums and flute instruments, parades, and animal sacrifices.

FIGURE 6-8   *Funerary Mask*
Larco Museum, Lima, Peru

FIGURE 6-9   *Burial Mask*
Larco Museum, Lima, Peru

FIGURE 6-10   *Festival Mask*
Coca Museum, Puno, Peru

Part 4.
National Social Studies Standards:

The National Social Study Standard I Culture states: Social Studies programs should include experiences that provide for the study of culture and cultural diversity so the learner can:

- Explore and describe similarities and differences in ways groups, societies, and cultures address similar human needs and concerns;
- Compare ways in which people from different cultures deal with their physical environment and social conditions; and
- Describe ways in which language, stories, folktales, music and artistic creations serve as expressions of culture and influence behavior of people living in a particular culture.

National Visual Arts Standards:

- Connecting: VA: Cn10.1.4a: Create works of art that reflect community cultural traditions.
- Connecting: VA: Cn11.1.4a: Through observation, infer information about time, place, and culture in which a work was created.
- Creating: VA: Cr2.1.4a: Explore and invent art making techniques and approaches.

Part 5.
Geographical Regions of the Native American Cultures

This Native American unit includes the geographical regions of the United States: Eastern, Plains, Southwest, and Northwest.

The theme *People and the Environment* includes the following subtopics: Land and Climate; Animals; Clothing; Food / Crops; Architecture and Tools / Transportation.

The theme *People in Society* includes the following subtopics: People, Origins and Language; Political and Social Structure; Economy; Games and Sports; Achievements and Historical Events.

The theme *People and Their Beliefs* includes the following subtopics: Beliefs; Myths / Literature; Rituals / Ceremonies; Dance / Regalia; Music / Instruments and Art / Materials.

SUMMARY OF TEAM MEETING

At the conclusion of the meeting, each teacher reviewed the material, geographical regions, and the themes that were selected. All teachers agreed to present the three themes to students in an introductory lesson with an art activity.

- Margaret selected the Northwest region and theme, *People and Beliefs.*
- Leah chose the Southwest region and theme, *People and the Environment.*
- Colleen selected the Eastern region and theme, *People and the Environment.*
- Tamara selected the Plains region and theme, *People in Society.*

Tomorrow's meeting, Tuesday at the same time, each teacher will present their lesson idea and art activities for the unit. The research worksheet passed out at the end of the meeting assists with lesson ideas.

RESEARCH WORKSHEET	NOTES
Question: What resources are found in the environment and how are or were they used by people for survival?	
Theme 1: People and the Environment	
Land and climate	
Animals	
Clothing	
Food/crops	
Architecture	
Tools/Transportation	
Question: What are or were the various roles the individual plays in the social and political structure and contributions?	
Theme 2: People in Society	
People, Origins, and Language	
Political and Social Structure	
Economy	
Games and Sports	
Achievements	
Historical Events	
Question: What are or were the belief systems; and how are or were they manifested in other areas?	
Theme 3: People and Their Beliefs	
Beliefs	
Myths/Literature	
Rituals/Ceremonies	
Dance/Regalia	
Music/Instruments	
Art/Materials	

TUESDAY'S TEAM MEETING

The following material is the introductory lesson for all fourth-grade classes using the theme *People and the Environment.* This content aligns itself with Social Studies standards.

INTRODUCTORY LESSON FOR UNIT: AMERICAN ROOTS

Essential Question

What resources are found in the environment and how are or were they used by people for survival in this culture?

Objectives: The student will:

- Identify the major regions of North American early Native Americans.
- Create artwork that depicts environmental characteristics of a region: climate, land, and animals (6-11).

Lesson Presentation

A PowerPoint presentation introduces a map of the United States that displays the labeled four geographical regions. As this visual presentation continues, each region is presented to the students and contains environmental images and bulleted text describing the land, climate, and animals that inhabit the area.

Art Materials:

Drawing paper 8" x 8"
Pencil, eraser, ruler, crayons
PowerPoint program
Environmental visuals

FIGURE 6-11

Artwork depicting the Northwest region.

Art Language

Space has background, middleground, and foreground.
Pattern is created by the repetition of lines, shapes, and colors.
Proportion is the size relationship between shapes.
Focal Point is the major emphasis in an artwork.

Assessment: Criteria for Artwork

1. Two or more animals placed in the artwork
2. Characteristic of the region selected by student
3. Self-portrait placed in center of the art as focal point of the artwork
4. Spatial characteristics include:
   - Land has background, middleground, and foreground
   - Change of sizes, large images in the front, smaller in background
   - Overlapped shapes
   - Bright colors in the front, dull colors in the back

AMERICAN ROOTS – OVERVIEW OF INDIVIDUAL CLASSROOM LESSONS

FIGURE 6-12

Margaret selected the Northwest region and theme, *People and Beliefs.*

Essential Question: *What are or were the belief systems; and how are or were they manifested in other areas?*

Focus: Mythology of Origin of Totem Animals

Art Project: Students select an animal as their original totem (6-12).

Assessment: Completed drawing of animal and imaginative written myth about their animal.

Leah chose Southwest region and theme, *People and the Environment.*

Essential Question: *What resources are found in the environment and how are or were they used by people for survival?*

Focus: Weaving Process (6-13): From Sheep to Yarn

Art Project: Students weave a wall hanging using yarn and cardboard loom.

Assessment: Completed weaving, off the loom and hanging on wall. Students identify the steps for making yarn on worksheet

Colleen selected the Eastern region and theme, *People and the Environment.*

Essential Question: *What resources are found in the environment and how are or were they used by people for survival?*

Focus: Pottery-making

Art Project: Students using clay techniques make bowl with geometric patterns (6-14).

Assessment: Pottery form is well made with clean incised designs. Students identify clay terms in fill-in-the-blank worksheet.

Tamara selected the Plains region and theme *People in Society.*

Essential question: *What are or were the various roles the individual plays in the social and political structure and contributions?*

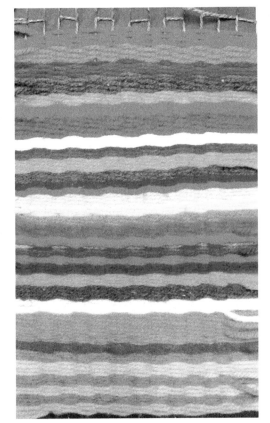

FIGURE 6-13

NOTES

FIGURE 6-14

ART FOR THE ELEMENTARY EDUCATOR

NOTES

Focus: Symbols used as a communication technique (6-15).

Art Project: Students create a story using symbols used by the Plains Indian.

Assessment: Artwork is completed and students write the story they made in symbols.

Documentation: The following material is based upon the research for Native Americans of the Plains using the three themes:

People and the Environment
Land and Climate: Grassy Land, Snowy in Winter, Hot in Summer
Animals: Buffalo, Deer, Elk, Bear, Beaver, Porcupine, Antelope, Wolves
Clothing: Made from buffalo skin, Parfleche, Feathers Used For Headdress
Food/Crops: Major source was buffalo
Architecture: Tipi Made from Buffalo Skin
Tools/Transportation: Scrapers, Bows and Arrows, Awls, Horse Pulling Travois, Cradle Board for Children

People in Society
People, Origins, and Language: Famous Tribes of Great Plains Indians: Blackfoot, Cheyenne, Pawnee, Crow, Comanche, Arapaho, Lakota
Language: Lakota, Algonquian, Symbols drawn on skin recording events
Political and Social Structure: Chiefdom, Tribes, Clans

Economy: Barter	
Games and Sports: Hand and Foot Ball Game, Hoop and Pole	
Achievements: Hunters, Heroic Leaders, Horse Culture	
Historical Events: Battle of Little Big Horn	

People and Their Beliefs
Beliefs: The Great Spirit, Vision Quest, Animism, Shaman
Myths/Literature: Tricksters, Creation Myth, How the World Was Made
The Legend of the Peace Pipes, Songs of the Buffalo Hunt, Songs of the Birds
Rituals/Ceremonies: Sundance, Smudging Rituals, Medicine Bag
Dance/Regalia: Pow Wow, Ghost Dance
Music/Instruments: Drums, Shakers
Art/Materials: Drawing War Battles on Skin, Shields for Protection, Beading on Clothing, Designs on Tipi's and Parfleche

Ideas for Art Projects Based Upon Themes

Theme: Environment: Landscape with animals
- A Buffalo Hunt
- Designs on a 3-D Tipi
- The Making of a Clay Buffalo
- The Drawing of a Feather

Theme: Society: Portrait of Famous Chief
- An Illustration for an Original Poem
- The Battle of Little Big Horn
- Designs on a War Shield
- War Designs on a Self-Portrait
- Symbols as a Communication Tool

Theme: Beliefs: Designs on the Shape of a Drum
- Medicine Bag
- Geometric Designs on Parfleche
- Images That Represent a Myth

Day Seven: Tuesday

LEWANDA'S CLASSROOM
FIRST GRADE

Tick Tock, Goes the Clock
What time is it?
I ask the clock
It's 2 o'clock, says the Clock
Tick Tock

MORNING NOTES, RIGHT BEFORE THE BELL

What Time Is It? This phrase is a rhyme I made up on the way to school to be part of the afternoon's math lesson. Yesterday, Sharlene gave me some ideas about writing the *Time* lesson and how to make the lesson exciting for the students. She suggested using an interactive approach by having students recite a rhyme while using an art project. She handed me material on the steps for crafting a large paper clock and said, "*Since the project is about time, why not have students make a clock, with movable hands, and have students move to a rhyme to tell time?*" Sharlene recapped the benefits of this lesson by addressing learning styles. The audio component is embraced when the students recite the rhyme, and body movement to the rhyme involves the kinesthetic aspect. The art project, making the clock, incorporates the visual and kinesthetic features of learning styles.

LUNCH NOTES ON THE RHYME

I designed some simple body movements to match the time rhyme while munching on my sandwich during lunch. I'm going to introduce the math lesson this afternoon.

Movement suggestions for this rhyme can be viewed on page 192.

Tick Tock, Goes the Clock
What time is it?
I ask the clock
It's 2 o'clock, says the Clock
Tick Tock

MATH LESSON
Essential Questions

Why is it important to tell time?
Can you describe a clock?
How would you describe time?

On one wall are the essential questions, and on the other wall are laminated posters listing the elements and principles of art. I placed arrows next to the art words we use in all our classroom art projects.

ART VOCABULARY

Geometric shapes are circles, rectangles, and free-form
Lines are Vertical, Horizontal, Straight
Colors are used for seasonal activities, warm, cool
Patterns are made when repeating lines, shapes, and colors

Students are shown via PowerPoint presentation a variety of clock styles. While viewing the presentation, the students agree on the common characteristic of all clocks, such as telling time, the hands, and the numbers. To introduce the concept of time, students are asked to share activities they did yesterday, which is in the past; today, which is in the present; and activities they plan to do tomorrow, which is in the future.

The next part of this lesson is to have students practice reciting the rhyme with body movements by following the teacher's directions. Once the students are proficient with the rhyme and movements, the teacher writes different times on the board: 2 o'clock, 6 o'clock, 8 o'clock, and 11 o'clock.

While the students perform the rhyme, the teacher points to a clock number on the board and the students call out the time. This active enterprise is performed for all the "times." After the rhyme session, students are excited to hear that during this math lesson today, we will be making play paper clocks.

FIGURE 7-1

National Standards

National Math Standard:
• *First Grade:* Students will tell and write time.

National Visual Arts Standards:
• Creating: VA: CR1.C1.1 a: Engage collaboratively in exploration and imaginative play with materials.
• Responding: VA: Re.7.2.1a: Compare images that represent the same subject.

Objectives: The student will:

• Recognize specific times and parts of a clock.
• Identify specific times on a clock.
• Create a paper clock with numbers, hours, and minute hands.

Vocabulary

Time is how we look at our life, the past, the present, and our future using hours, minutes, and seconds.
A *clock* is a device for presenting time with big and little hands and numbers.

Art Materials:

Tag board 10"round for the clock face
Tag board for clock's big and little hands
Precut circle shapes for the clock center for students to trace and cut out
Pre-cut shapes for clock's hands for students to trace
Construction paper
Crayons
Pencils
Glue
Scissors
Brass prong paper file fasteners ½ inch
(placed in the clock's center by teacher)
PowerPoint presentation: Examples of different types of clocks

Steps for making art project:

Art materials are passed out to the students. As the teacher demonstrates the steps on the board, the students follow the directions.

1. Trace the precut pattern of the circle and the clock's hands with a pencil and cut out both shapes.
2. Following the teacher's directions, students use crayons and
   - write the number 12 at the top of the circle,
   - write the number 6 at the bottom of circle,
   - on the right side between 12 and 6, write 3,
   - on the left side between 6 and 12, write 9.
3. Looking at the clock sample on the board students write in the numbers 1, 2, 4, 5, 7, 8, 10, and 11.
4. Insert in the center of the clock the hands with the brass fastener with help from the teacher, so the hands can move.

FIGURE 7-2

5. Design variations:
   - Clock centers can be used to illustrate additional classroom themes such as seasons, pattern designs, family portraits, landscapes, and imaginary creatures.
   - To change the clocks into wristwatches, the two straps can be extended and decorated, then glued to the edges of the clock. Include three to four holes on one strap and the shape of a fastener on the other strap.

FIGURE 7-3

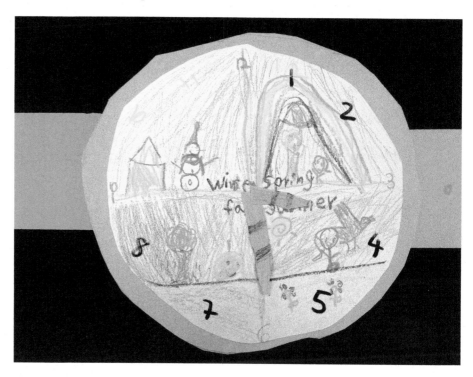

Assessment

The students:
1. Verbally identified parts of a clock.
2. Verbally identified the clock's time written on the board while performing the rhyme.
3. Identified time using the clock worksheet by drawing the hands on the clocks.
4. Completed artwork with numbers, hours, and minute hands.

NAME: _____   What Time Is It?

Draw the hands that match the time.

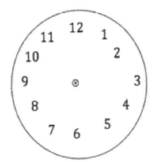

TIME: 2:00

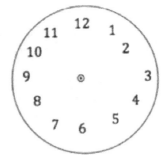

TIME: 8:30

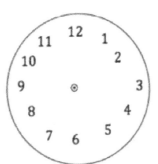

TIME: 10:15

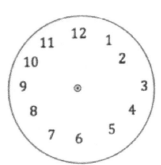

TIME: 11:45

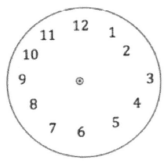

TIME: 4:00

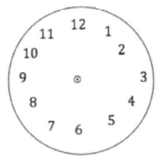

TIME: 6:00

STRATEGIES FOR MOTIVATING STUDENTS

All educators want their students to be successful in all learning situations. An important ingredient in the teaching process is conducting an effective motivation that encourages students' participation. When a teacher stimulates students to take action and perform, that arouses an intrinsic desire to participate; and that drive is called motivation. In the classroom, if the students are smiling, laughing, and impatient to get started on an activity the teacher has successfully motivated the students' curiosity, the desire to learn, explore, and play.

The following material is a collection of guidelines to recall when motivating students:

1. Create a relaxed and enjoyable atmosphere in the classroom by playing music as the students arrive in the morning. Participate and lead students in body movements to music that has a rhythmic tempo. According to research, using music, lighting, color, and aroma can improve academic achievement by enhancing a person's ability to retain information.

2. As students listen intensely to a story the teacher is narrating, they recollect the story (beginning, middle, and end) because of the interrelated content, thus helping the brain to remember. Students enjoy stories and when they become emotionally involved, they are motivated to develop a positive attitude toward learning. Storytelling, a stimulating medium, enhances student's imagination by visualizing, thus creating images in their mind.

3. An effective teaching tool and motivator is the use of visual imagery such as posters, photographs, picture books, videos, Internet images, graphic organizers, and PowerPoint presentations. The majority of students learn using visual–spatial intelligence along with open-ended discussions. Visual learning is valuable because it is groundwork for supporting students' language development. When designing PowerPoint presentations, it is important for each color slide to display an image along with bulleted text used as a guide for class discussion. Incorporating slides that ripple, bounce, zoom, spiral, and flip, along with sounds, offer "bells and whistles" certain to entertain and captivate the young viewer.

4. Students involved in the creative process embrace a variety of phases. As students begin their creative activity, their previous knowledge will influence what their artistic response will be. Students will demonstrate enthusiasm to accomplish the activity motivated by the teacher's instructional strategies. Exploration of materials and tools will enhance the students' skill level as they become immersed in the activity, because students are asking themselves questions, trying out ideas, and deciding what actions to take for the project. When introducing motivation, the teacher can

present images to students to help them recall past experiences or conduct a discussion to explore student's feelings and imagination. During the creative process, students need enough time to complete their art activity. Those students who are hesitant or feel self-doubting about their work can be encouraged by the teacher's suggestions, questions, and verbal praise.

Day Eight: Wednesday

ESTHER'S CLASSROOM
THIRD GRADE

MORNING NOTES, RIGHT BEFORE THE BELL

Interesting! I received an e-mail this morning from Sharlene, the art teacher. She asked everyone to select one work of art, download and print it, then remember to bring it to our second art workshop today after school.

FIGURE 8-1

Realism: Art that represents the natural world – what you see!

FIGURE 8-2

Nonobjective/Formalism: *Art created using only the Elements and Principles of Art.*

FIGURE 8-4

Expressionism: *Art that evokes an emotional response by using the elements of color, shape, and spatial techniques.*

FIGURE 8-3

Abstract: *Art that distorts real-life images often using spatial or color elements.*

FIGURE 8-5

Surrealism: *Art that is a mixture of imagination—fanciful, dreamlike images with realistic characteristics.*

FACULTY ART WORKSHOP IN MEDIA CENTER

The following questionnaire was passed out to everyone, requesting that they complete the form as they view the work of art they selected earlier in the day.

State the Art Style: _____

1. What was the first thought in your mind as you looked at this work of art?

2. What were your feelings as you looked at the art?

3. Did the image bring back a memory for you?

4. Do you think this art is beautiful? If so, or if not, why?

5. What is your favorite feature of the art?

6. What do you think the artist is trying to say in the artwork?

7. Can you create an original story about the artwork?

8. Would you want to have this artwork in your home?

9. Would you pick out the same artwork a year from now?

10. If you were the artist, what would you change?

ARTICLE ON AESTHETICS

Aesthetics in the Classroom

Author: Miwon Choe

When artists create an image, an object of beauty, or any artifact of a symbolic nature, they are making a creative proposal that reflects their views of art and its significance. Some artists may focus on capturing the beauty of nature as seen in our eyes. Some may be interested in creating the finest arrangement of visual elements that appeals to our senses, even with the absence of recognizable objects. Others believe in expressing the experience of emotion as a primary source of creative inspiration. Yet another group of artists may utilize their images to communicate ideas and beliefs inspired by a broader social and political context. These artistic proposals invariably extend a special invitation to the world outside, meant to engage the viewers' responses and reactions.

So, we begin to wonder about these big questions: What makes an object art? How do we know which types of art are more artistic than other types? What is considered beautiful in one personal, social, and cultural context may appear untrue in another setting or a different time period.

So, could we say art and beauty may be two sides of the same coin depending on the eyes of the beholder? What if the art objects challenge our assumptions and beliefs about beauty? Does artistic merit have to include beautiful objects in life? An object or image might speak of a social agenda or conceptual ideas rather than representing visual skills, but could we still consider it to be art?

This is where the big "A" for aesthetics becomes an important topic of discussion when we are learning about art. Dr. Laura Chapman, a writer and prominent art educator based in Cincinnati, Ohio, once stated that Aesthetics (also known as esthetics) is almost an opposite experience of "An-esthetics." From Greek origin, "an" refers to without and "esthetics" to sensation. Aesthetics would then refer to being without sensation.

Experiencing art, either through creating, viewing, or working with various art media, requires more than what meets the eye and visual skills.

There is a deeply felt experience inside us that triggers emotional responses or intellectual reactions. It is what makes us uniquely human. We respond to beauty, because it elevates our senses to a place of being happy, content, memorable, or even fun, thus motivating us to come back for more.

Contributed by Miwon Choe. Copyright © Kendall Hunt Publishing Company.

I recall experiences of standing at the edge of the Grand Canyon looking down at the majestic sunken valley, a breathtaking view of the sunset on a Bermuda beach, a beautiful lifesize painting of Pierre-Auguste Renoir at Musée d'Orsay in Paris, France. The concept of time stops when we have such moments of extraordinary encounter in life. Chapman's view of aesthetics seems a bit tongue in cheek and humorous, but she entertains the idea that aesthetic experience is possible when we are able to feel with our senses. These special feelings may be experienced not only through visual arts, music, dance, and theatre, but also through extraordinary experiences of ordinary events.

Now there is another set of questions we can ponder about aesthetics. Even with our senses and tastes fully accompanying us, how do we determine something is or isn't art?

Is there a uniform measuring apparatus, or theory of aesthetics? Do we merely exercise our discretionary judgment beyond the reasonable doubt? The Western perspectives attempt to answer these big questions in terms of value-driven philosophical inquiry, where we use our thinking capacity to determine how we perceive art and beauty. In this view, artistic merit is assigned by the theme of the artistic proposal, and the manner in which it communicates to us. These artistic merits may be referred to as aesthetic stances.

Imitationalism

One of the aesthetic stances we are most familiar with is the art that mirrors the physical world in which we live. This is one of the oldest theories of art written by the Greek philosopher Plato, that art is an imitation of all the living things and nature around us. Plato stated, initially as a critical view of art, that art imitates the objects and events of ordinary life, and therefore is not as original or significant as the real things that exist. We can still question what counts as real in our experience, but we tend to think that a picture must be a picture of what we see, and that a good artist can make a picture that will look just like the real objects.

When we hear most people lamenting that they can't draw, they really mean "not realistic as the way things appear in the visual world." Frequently, the person is thought to be talented when the exact copy of the real world is presented in art. It is natural that children learn by imitating what they see and hear from an adult world. Gradually, they pick and choose as they develop preferences. Likewise, for most artists who depict things and nature in a realistic manner, they select a certain aspect of reality or things to add which enrich their creative style. This artistic preference and point of view still plays an important part within the imitation theory of aesthetics.

American female artist, Georgia O'Keefe (1887–1986), decided to create large-format paintings of close-up flowers as if seen through a magnifying glass. Here's what she tells us about her painting:

> "When you take a flower in your hand and really look at it, it's your world for the moment. I want to give that world to someone else. However, if I could paint the flower exactly as I see it, no one would see what I see, because I would paint it small like the flower is small. So I said to myself - I'll paint what I see, what the flower is to me, but I'll paint it big and they will be surprised into taking time to look at it - I will make even busy New Yorkers take time to see what I see of flowers."

Expressionism

The second aesthetic stance is a compelling one, because we can easily acknowledge that feelings are inevitably tied to art. Expressionist artists seek to express meaning and emotional experience rather than representing the external visual world as seen through our eyes. We recognize this stance when artworks primarily convey and trigger strong feelings or moods within us. The Expressionist art movement began in the modern 20th-century context when artists started looking inside as a reason for creating art. So, Expressionist art is meant to come from within the artist, reflecting the internal and psychological realities of modern life.

Expressionist artists exaggerate or distort the forms and shapes, and employ bold colors as important visual tools. A swirling sense of movement, restless brushstrokes, and gyrating lines in a repetitious pattern contribute to the emotionally charged state of the artist responding to anxieties, and lost feelings of living in a modern, industrial world.

Dutch artist Vincent van Gogh (1853–1890) writes about this Expressionist view of his paintings:

> "Look at the sky. It's not dark and black and without character. The black is, in fact deep blue. And over there, lighter blue and blowing through the blues and blackness the winds swirling through the air and then shining, burning, bursting through, the stars! You see how they roar their light. I don't know anything with certainty, but seeing the stars makes me dream... My emotions are sometimes so strong that I work without knowing it. The strokes in my paintings come like speech."

Formalism

The third aesthetic stance comes from Formalism. The form or formal quality in this context refers to the way artworks are represented with compositional art elements such as color, line, shape, texture, and other design principles, movement, variety, proportion, harmony, and so forth, rather than images of the physical world in a representational manner. In the paintings that emphasize formalistic aesthetics, artists focus on intrinsic values that exist in the visual elements and organization of them on canvas.

Frequently, no recognizable objects are included, yet the parts of the work fit together like a puzzle and demonstrate an effective use of the chosen art elements. It is believed that the origins of formalism are deeply rooted in ancient thought that the universe is governed by numerical relationships and patterns.

Modern formalism evolved during the late 19th and early 20th centuries. In this view, the value and merit of artwork is measured by the artist's abilities to apply formal elements in their artwork in an aesthetically pleasing manner. The formalist scholars claim that all art must have this formal quality in order for it to be true art, because the formal quality serves as a fundamental language that is shared by all works of art. We are applying formalistic art theory when we use basic art elements; color, line, shape, texture, and composition, to determine the value, style, and merit of the artwork. An American artist of the late 19th century, James Whistler (1834–1903) explains this formalistic view of aesthetics as the following:

> *"Nature contains the elements, in color and form, of all pictures, as the keyboard contains the notes of all music. But the artist is born to pick, and choose, and group with science, these elements, that the result may be beautiful – as the musician gathers his notes, and forms his chords, until he brings forth harmony."*

Alternative Viewpoints of Art and Aesthetics

The above three aesthetic theories attempt to explain what art is and what makes it beautiful. Critics argue, however, that the imitational, expressive, and formalistic definitions of art primarily address the Western view of aesthetics, and therefore do not include the art and aesthetic views of Asia, Africa, Latin America, the Islamic world, and various indigenous groups of the world. Their culture, worldviews, and the idea of beauty are not necessarily associated with the Western views of aesthetics.

Rather than the intrinsic value of form (Formalism), visual representation (Imitationalism), or expression of internal experience (Expressionism), the art forms in the non-Western art world are embedded in their unique cultural contexts and utility in their social functions. Therefore, the importance of art and idea of beauty would be determined based on the instrumental, ritual, and cultural significance practiced in a broader social and human context. Many scholars view that this alternative view of aesthetics is rooted in the anthropological view of art, where ritualistic and functional objects in a human context have meaning beyond simple description of formal elements, and the way art is presented to communicate its beauty.

So, the artifacts and material objects are considered not merely aesthetic items of beauty, but valued by the bigger role they play in the beliefs, rituals, and lives of people. These objects and artifacts include sculpture, masks, paintings, textiles, baskets, pots, tools, and even architecture. The meaning and significance of the objects are intimately associated with their unique symbol system and cultural patterns, as well as artistic techniques and materials.

In 1974, local farmers while digging a well outside the city of Xi'an in China, made one of the most extraordinary archeological discoveries in the world. They found thousands of clay soldiers in a trench like corridor underground. The farmers' discovery prompted further archeological investigation that ultimately revealed the ancient mausoleum of the first Emperor of China, Qin Shi Huang. These terracotta figures are life-sized, varying in height, each with unique individual facial features, positioned according to their ranks. Archeologists believe that these terracotta sculpture figures are the armies of Emperor Qin and they are part of funeral art forms buried in 210–209 BCE.

The job of these lifesize soldiers poised for battle was to protect the Emperor Qin in his afterlife, which reflects the ancient Chinese thoughts on death not being the end of life, but the beginning of life in another world. So, let's say we could perhaps ask a big "A" question here: Are these funeral figures considered art? What is the aesthetic significance of the Terracotta Army? Are they art because of their anatomically accurate representation of a real life figure (Imitationalism)? Does the compositional use of the formal elements make them art (Formalism)? Are they art because they express meaning and the emotional experience of the internal world (Expressionism)?

We could perhaps discuss all of these aesthetic theories in some limited measure, but the true value and significance of these clay sculptures lies in the cultural context on death and living in ancient China, as well as their aesthetic representations. So, the knowledge and understanding of the historical and social context of the ancient Chinese, rites of death rituals, helps us think critically and aesthetically beyond the boundaries of our own familiar experience.

When we look at artifacts created by specific cultural groups, we need to consider the value of such artifacts, by why and how they functioned within the particular cultural settings. This alternative aesthetics view is grounded on an anthropological view of art, where ritualistic and functional objects, in a human context, are considered aesthetically meaningful beyond simple description. In this view, how art objects fit into a culture's social practices is more important than the way art is presented to communicate its beauty.

Final Thought on Aesthetics

We create, view, and respond to art because of what art does to us, the way we feel and how we think about things, people, and the world outside. Some say art helps brighten the day, inspire happy feelings, and presents new ways of looking at things in life. Some say art is valued because it helps make meaningful connections with the world outside oneself. We also appreciate art for what it communicates to us; beauty, ideas, and thoughts. Art provides an avenue to express, some say for its own sake, yet art becomes far more significant when those expressions are being communicated to a wider audience.

The aesthetic theories and perspectives may be confusing, and all the lines of distinction seem to blur when it comes to determining what is art and beauty. It simply means that those standards of beauty and definition of art are relative to our own individual perspectives and creative experiences of art. So, the question of "What is art?" or "What is beauty?" could really be a question of "What is art to YOU?" and "What is beauty to YOU?" Therefore, our response to art becomes a personal adventure, journey, and inquiry as we create a unique individual version of our own aesthetics.

This article was written by Dr. Miwon Choe, an associate professor, and art education program coordinator at Western Kentucky University. She teaches undergraduate and graduate art education courses and delivers arts and humanities workshops for visual arts in-service teachers. She coordinates many P-12 visual arts outreach programs, including VSA New Understanding, ESL Art, Home School Art Alliance, Summer SCATS Art, and Super Saturday Art Programs.

Dr. Choe also serves as a faculty sponsor for the student exchange program between WKU and Hanyang University, Korea, and is a project leader of the Arts and Literacy program with Cuban teachers and students. Dr. Choe is a recipient of the 2014 WKU Potter College Faculty Award for her distinguished service work. Presently, she sponsors a Community Art Program, "Create" in Prinar del Rio, Cuba, conducting art workshops for faculty and students.

EXAMINING THE AESTHETICS OF A CULTURE

When studying the aesthetics of cultural images, what can it tell you about the culture? Review the following works of art and answer the following questions at the end of the images.

FIGURE 8-6

Zulu Wooden Dish with Animal, Africa

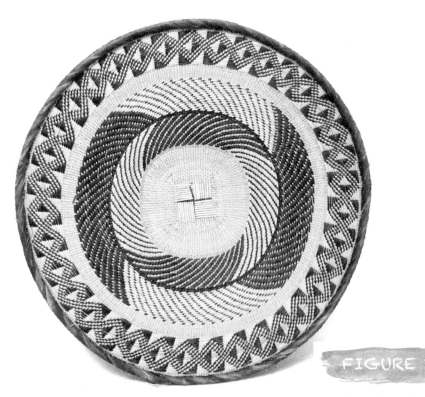

FIGURE 8-7

Zulu Basket, Africa

Dragon Tile, China

FIGURE 8-8

Terra Cotta Warrior, China

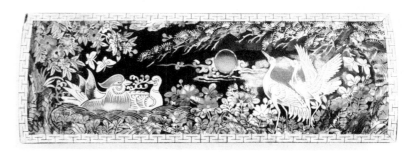

Shell Inlay Box, South Korea

Celedon Vase, South Korea

FIGURE 8-12   *Drum, Native American of the Plains*

FIGURE 8-13   *Feather & Bone Shaker, Native American of the Plains*

FIGURE 8-14   *Mayan Profile in Wood*

FIGURE 8-15   *Mayan Clay Sculpture*

Flower Tile, Turkey

FIGURE 8-17 Flower Plate, Turkey

Incan Wooden
Painted Plate

FIGURE 8-19 Incan god, Viracocha,
Relief in Clay

FIGURE 8-20 *Japanese Painting*

FIGURE 8-21 *Japanese Metal Plate*

FIGURE 8-22 *Turtle in Wood, Australia*

FIGURE 8-23 *Storytelling Plate on Wood, Australia*

ART FOR THE ELEMENTARY EDUCATOR

After reviewing the cultural images, answer the following questions.

- Does the artwork from the same culture exhibit an art style (i.e., Realism, Abstract, etc.)? If so, describe the style.
- Compare and contrast two cultural images.
- Is there any similarly in the subject matter or material found in the cultural images?
- Are the same features repeated in the works of art (i.e., line patterns, flowers, bright colors, neutral colors highly textural and symmetrical in balance)?
- Write a story about a selected cultural image.
- What role did a selected work of art play in the culture? Explain your answer (i.e., functional, ceremonial, decoration, storytelling, idea or ethos of a nation).

Day Nine: Thursday

LYNN'S CLASSROOM
FIFTH GRADE

MORNING NOTES, BEFORE FIRST PERIOD

A new student arrived this morning. He was acting bashful and appeared nervous. Oktay just recently moved to the United States from Turkey and only speaks a little English. After all the students arrived in the classroom, I assigned Logan, the room's "diplomat," to be his buddy and to show him around the school. In each classroom, there is a "diplomat" who is assigned to escort and get new students acquainted to the school's schedule. The diplomat program has been effective when welcoming new students by creating a friendly and comfortable atmosphere. Oktay has been assigned to my class and has arrived in time for the introduction of the Social Studies unit on ancient civilizations.

SOCIAL STUDIES UNIT – ANCIENT CIVILIZATIONS
National Social Studies Standards:

- NSS-Wh.5-12.3 Era 3: Classical Traditions, Major Religions, Giant Empires 1000–300 BCE
- *How Major Religions and Large-Scale Empires Arose in the Mediterranean Basin, China, and India, 500–300 BCE.*

An excellent resource for teaching this Social Studies, World History unit is a well-designed resource book, *Teacher Created Resources* by author Julia Mc-Means. The book contains reading strategies, content-specific vocabulary, multiple assessment options, activities for various learning styles, and graphic organizers. The book's contents include: Unit 1 Ancient Civilizations, Unit 2 Ancient Egypt, Unit 3 China, Unit 4 India, and Unit 5 Ancient Greece.

Resource:

McMeans, Julia. (2010). *Differentiated Lessons and Assessments*: Social Studies. Retrieved on February 28, 2015 from https://books.google.com/books

National Visual Arts Standards:

- Creating: VA: Cr 1.1.5a: Combine ideas to generate an innovative idea for art making.
- Responding: VA: Re. 7.2. 5a: Identify and analyze cultural associations suggested by visual imagery.
- Connecting: VA.Cn11.15a: Identify how art is used to inform or change beliefs, values, or behaviors of an individual or society.

Essential Questions

Why is it important to learn about different cultures?
What can you say about symbolism?
What conclusions can you draw about the relationship between images and beliefs?

Introduction of Art Project: Background

The word "mandala" is an Indian word from Sanskrit meaning "circle." It is a symbol that represents wholeness. The mandala is seen in nature, in the earth, sun, and moon. The basic shapes of most mandalas are a square using a circle as center. Circles are also placed on all four sides as gates. The design demonstrates radial balance and symbolizes unity and harmony. Mandalas can also represent a connection between our personal world and our outer reality.

Designing a mandala can be both inspiring and relaxing and can symbolize what you would like to achieve in your life. Many different cultures around the world use mandalas in their spiritual practices. The Native Americans created the circular medicine wheel; the Aztec calendar was a circular timekeeper; and Tibetan monks created sand mandalas used as an aid in

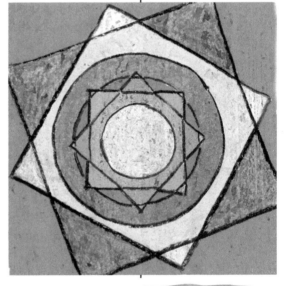

FIGURE 9-1

ART FOR THE ELEMENTARY EDUCATOR

meditation. Mandalas usually have a central point from which radiates an array of geometric and organic symbols and shapes. Geometric patterns have been used in artwork throughout history in many cultures—Greek, Roman, Byzantine, Central Asia, and Persian.

Geometry has been used in the planning of buildings such as churches, temples, mosques, and monuments. The use of geometric shapes such as a square, octagonal, and the star motif influenced Islamic art and architecture.

Objective: The student will:

- Produce a radial balance design using resist technique.
- Define art terminology.
- Connect the relationship of belief systems through images.

Vocabulary

Mandala means circle and is a symbol of wholeness and used for meditation and healing.
Symbol is a thing that represents or stands for something else, especially a material object representing something abstract.
Radial Balance is a design initiated at the center.
and can be divided into two identical halves.
Geometric Shape is a two-dimensional area with identifiable boundaries using an enclosed line.
Pattern is the repetition of shapes, lines, or colors.
Texture refers to the surface quality and the way things look or feel.
Overlapping Shapes is to extend or lie partly over another shape.
Resist Technique involves using two incompatible mediums to create layered effects with color and texture.
Complementary Colors are opposite on the color wheel.

Art Materials:

Precut geometric shapes: circles, squares, and triangles, variety of different sizes
Paper (tag paper is best) in shape of a square 12" x 12" or 10" x 10"
Pencil, oil pastels, brush (large, 3–4 inches)
Black tempera paint, diluted with water

Assessment:

1. The design fills the page and the resist technique does not dominate the image.
2. Worksheet completed with written definitions of the terms.

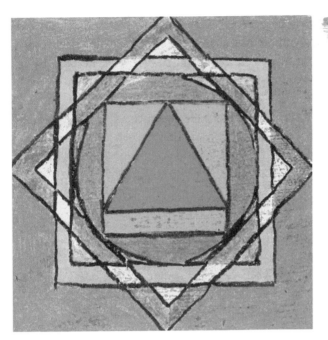

FIGURE 9-2

MANDALA ART PROJECT

1. Students selected a variety of geometric shapes of different sizes.
2. Teacher's example for planning the design:
   a. The largest geometric shape, a circle is placed on the square paper.
   b. A diamond is placed, inside the circle.
   c. A circle is placed inside the diamond.
   d. A triangle is placed inside that circle.
   e. A smaller circle is placed inside the tri angle.
   f. A smaller circle is placed inside the circle to complete the design.
3. Once the design is completed, the shapes are traced with a pencil.
4. Complementary colors are lightly written in the shapes. The same shapes are colored, blue, the same shapes are colored orange, etc.
5. The shapes are colored in using oil pastels.
6. After the design is completely filled in, a black oil pastel traces all shapes.
7. The design is lightly painted with the diluted Tempera black paint.

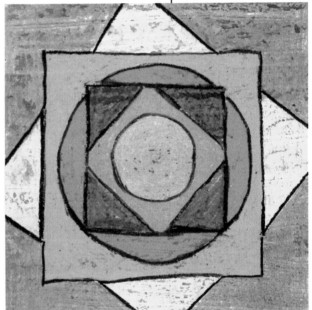

FIGURE 9-3

ART FOR THE ELEMENTARY EDUCATOR

NOTES

ART ASSESSMENT WORKSHEET

Define the following terms.

Mandala
Symbol
Radial Balance
Geometric Shapes
Pattern
Texture
Overlapping Shapes
Resist Technique
Complementary Colors
Name a culture that observes the mandala.
Review the function sand symbolism of the mandala?

LUNCH BREAK NOTES

A colleague in our school is an excellent resource on the theme of cultural diversity and has presented at many conferences. I approached her during lunch with information about the new student, and asked for some material to assist me. She will be sending me an article at the end of the day.

Building Culturally Diverse Classrooms
Author: Sandra Bird

The challenge of building culturally diverse learning environments for children begins with the teachers of these students. It requires an examination of the biases and prejudices that teachers can, and most likely do, bring with them. Taking a step toward recognizing our own human limitations will help to ensure that our students will be more accepted for "who they are," not "who we want them to be." Graeme Chalmers (1997) in his monograph, *Celebrating Pluralism: Art, Education, and Cultural Diversity,* succinctly envisioned the realities and resulting responsibilities that teachers face in 21st-century classrooms. "My ideas are based upon a few general premises: that cultural pluralism is a reality and that reluctant, grudging, or tacit recognition by one culture or another must be replaced by genuine appreciation and proactive corrective action; that no racial, cultural, or national group is inherently superior to another; that no one group's art [or anything else for that matter] is basically superior to another's; and that equality of opportunity, in the art classroom and elsewhere, is a right that must be enjoyed by every student regardless of ethnic, cultural, or other differences" (p. 2).

Teachers must look for ways to make all children in their classrooms feel safe. Being able to highlight our human similarities and differences teaches children to be more observant (a common goal of any subject matter), as well as being more empathetic (a quality of character relevant to all people in all circumstances). The realities of our age stretch the "norm" we thought we knew. In doing so, we make learning so much more intimately related to the real lives of all of our students.

The following case study, reflecting on 7-year-old Oktay, exemplifies these points fairly well. When this Turkish immigrant entered the American classroom, he was at an extreme disadvantage for a lack of being able to master English as a second language. The idea of pairing him with a "buddy" who speaks his language will not be as easily realized as it would be for our dominant second language speakers of Spanish.

The likelihood of a paraprofessional aiding Oktay with translations is fairly slim, and he would have to carry an electronic translator with him to all classes until he picks up a "working" English. He will try very hard to fit in with the other children, but may not be able to overcome the language barrier for several years and this could seriously delay his academic development.

Oktay's troubles were only just starting with the obstacle of language, as many of the other children in his classroom carry misconceptions about the religion he practices, the foods he brings from home for his lunches, or even the games he tries to play at recess. So little is accurately known about Islamic cultures in America, and these prejudices have only become worse since the tragedy of 9-11. Some teachers are afraid to mention anything related to Islam for fear they might be accused of trying to convert the children to a religious faith. Some Muslim students in America have gone through their entire educational sequence without ever hearing anything positive about their culture of origin. Learning about the multiple perspectives in religions and philosophies (of all types) can only help to repair the misconceptions that persist in our current age.

One might ask if it is his teacher's fault for not speaking his language or accurately knowing his cultural norms—the truth is the world is a pretty big place and knowing everything about every origin would certainly be a super-human expectation. Still, that lack of knowledge on the part of the teacher could be dramatically changed if the teacher attempted to fill that gap. Learning and using a simple greeting, such as "Gunaydin Oktay" (Good morning, Oktay), could make a world of difference in the eyes of this boy. His language could become a part of his classroom experience and thereby help him to recognize that he is a valuable member of his class. Perhaps Oktay's parents might be invited to class one day to share some of the cultural objects from their home.

Oktay's father served as a guard at the Topkapi Museum in Istanbul. He might wear his former uniform to class one day and show photographs of this exciting Ottoman palace complex and the wonderful art objects that can be viewed there. Or maybe Oktay's mother is an excellent baker of baklava, and a math and science lesson in this class might involve sharing this delicious pastry. Later she could teach the students how to make baklava using a recipe involving the transposition of the metric system to the measuring system commonly used in America.

Having Oktay's parents in the class will not teach the students everything they need to know about Turkish culture and history, but it will begin to build a cognitive schema that is based upon real experience and thus will be more reliable than reading a few cryptic pages in the Social Studies book.

Oktay and his parents reflect current culture in one Islamic country, Turkey. In fact they reflect current cultural realities shared in his little village of Harran within the southeastern corner of the country. The beauty of the village of Harran is that the well-known biblical figure of Abraham was born in that city many centuries ago. Throughout our history we discover an overlapping of our ancestries.

One day I am certain we will all find ourselves related to one another (if just being human is not enough). The classroom teacher should look toward each child and their parents as potential speakers related to the diversification of their classroom. Teachers can continue to participate in workshops, classes, and museum programs offered by universities, professional organizations, and other institutions. Another way that teachers can help to diversify their classrooms is to travel to places around the world that can help fill in some of their content gaps.

There are several travel grants and workshops available to teachers (a quick survey of topics such as "travel grants for teachers" on the Internet will identify several programs including Funds for Teachers, Fulbright-Hayes Seminars Abroad, American Councils for International Academic Exchanges...to name just a few). Local and regional outreach programs with cultural organizations can also provide in-depth discovery of the culture understudy, including histories, arts, sciences, and other ways of knowing our shared world. For more ideas on how to make your classroom diverse, please consult *Celebrating Pluralism* (Chalmers, 1997). The excellent list of interdisciplinary references on cultural diversity at the end of this monograph makes it well worth a place in your teaching library.

Sandra Bird, Ph.D., the Senior Art Educator within the School of Art and Design, at Kennesaw State University, wrote this article. Her areas of specialization include cross-cultural aesthetics (with emphasis on the Middle East and Africa), Islamic art history, and intercultural curriculum for university service learning projects within public schools. Her book Wisdom at the Crossroads, *chronicling a service learning curricular project in Turkey, was facilitated in a local elementary school in the Kennesaw, Georgia area. She is also currently working on a book focused on the arts of the Osun River in Nigeria.*

Day Ten: Friday

MARY'S CLASSROOM
KINDERGARTEN

AFTERNOON NOTES

I have a smile on my face. The students are drawing, coloring, and talking non-stop with their friends. What a difference from this morning! Besides the horrible weather, students came in looking tired, sleepy, and unresponsive during the morning's lessons.

Because the morning was so dismal, I decided to brighten up the afternoon for the students with an art project. I'll use this art project to review the Life Science lesson on flowers. Also, I am arranging students in teams to work cooperatively. Team activity encourages students to support each other's input and ideas so they can complete the art project entitled, "My Flower Garden." According to Kovalik and Olsen (1993), when students work in a group they are actively engaged, rather than being in a passive role, which increases understanding, thinking skills, and interaction and improves the quality of the project.

Each member of the group wears an art badge during the making of the art project. Titles on the art badges include: the *Checker*, making sure all members agree on decisions before they resume the work; the *Time Keeper*, who watches the clock telling others when they need to stop work and clean up; the *Manager* is responsible for collecting and putting art materials away; and throughout the art project, the *Whisperer* reminds others to lower voices and whisper when they are talk too loudly. A cooperative art project is an ideal opportunity to enhance students' social skills such as listening, sharing, encouraging each other, taking turns, and solving disagreements.

As students work in a team, they realize that they depend on each other to accomplish their goal—the completion of their artwork. When students participate in a cooperative project, this opportunity allows students to share their feelings and ideas, increase listening skills, and develop respect and patience when teammates have a different opinion.

Based on studies, when students participate in a cooperative learning situation the learning process is enhanced because students are actively participating, emotionally motivated, and developing the aptitude to accept another student's viewpoint.

FLOWER GARDEN ART PROJECT
Standards

Science Standards:
- K.L.1.2 Students are also expected to develop understanding of what plants and animals need to survive and the relationship between their needs and where they live.

National Visual Arts Standards:
- Creating: VA: Cr1.2.Ka: Engage collaboratively in creative art-making in response to an artistic problem.
- Creating: VA: Cr2.3.Ka: Create art that represents natural and constructed environments.

FIGURE 10-1

Objectives: The students will:

- Identify different parts of a plant and their functions.
- Work cooperatively to produce a drawing of a flower garden

Vocabulary

Roots help support the plant, and take in water and nutrients.
Leaves help plants use sunlight to make food.
Stems, Stalks, and *Trunks* support the plant so it can stand up.
Flowers on plants help with reproduction and can produce fruit and seeds.
Seeds aid in the reproduction of plants.

Essential Questions

Why do we learn about plants? Can you explain how the sun affects plants? Can you predict the outcome if a plant doesn't receive water?

Visual Resources

Parts of a Plant for Kids – Animation. (2011). Retrieved March 19, 2015 from *https://youtu.be/xO8hrqDuMmY*
The speakers have strong accents. If the accents are difficult to understand, present this YouTube without audio and teachers can tell the story. 7:39 minutes

FIGURE 10-2

Sid the Seed. (2009). Retrieved March 19, 2015 from https://youtu.be/uUmSnvJfzEg
Children's book story about a seed that grows up to be a tree and has two friends. A presentation that is charming, engaging, and beautifully illustrated. 5:21 minutes

Parts of a Flower. (2010).
Retrieved March 19, 2015 from https://youtu.be/sXrnHff2Kjc
Parts of a flower are repeated to music in a song arrangement. 1:21 minutes

Art Materials:

White drawing paper 24" x 36"
Pencils, markers, crayons
Visuals of flowers and bugs (use Internet for images)

Art Language

Line is the path of a moving dot through space and has more length than thickness.
Types of lines: Vertical, Horizontal, Diagonal, Zigzag, Curved, and Spiral
Shape is a two-dimensional area with identifiable boundaries using an enclosed line.
     Geometric shapes include Circle, Square, Rectangle, Oval, and Triangle.
Free-Form shapes are found in nature.
Color is what the eye sees when light is viewed directly or as reflected light, day-light contains light waves of all colors.
Pattern is the repetition of lines, colors, and shapes in artwork.

View additional movement ideas for this rhyme on page 194.

Flowers in
my garden

Flowers in my garden
grow short and tall.
With bugs that squirm,
hop, fly and crawl.
Flowers in my garden
grow colors bright
With stems and leaves
that love the light.

FLOWER GARDEN ART PROJECT

1. Students view the video on the parts of a plant and engage in a discussion afterwards.
2. Students are placed in teams of four and given a badge that identifies their responsibility: *Time Keeper, Manager, Checker,* and *Whisperer.*
3. Each team is given the drawing paper, positioned horizontally, and instructed to draw a line that represents the ground, from one side of the paper to the other.
4. The *Flower Garden Rhyme* is introduced to the students, who learn and repeat the rhyme while incorporating body movements.
5. Students then share what kind of bugs squirm, hop, fly, and crawl.
6. Students are told to draw four or more bugs in their flower garden and five or more flowers making sure they have flowers short and tall.

FIGURE 10-3

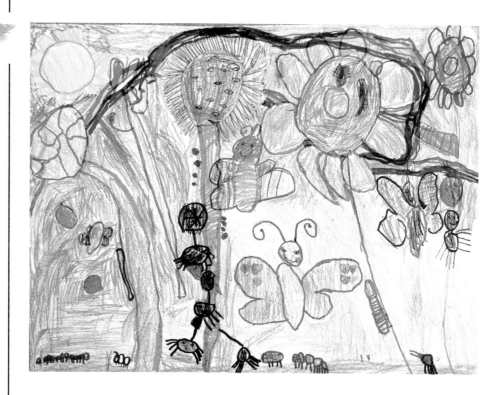

SCIENCE ASSESSMENT

NAME: _____

Write in the correct word.

Roots need _____ to drink.

Leaves need_____ to make _____.

Stems help flowers to _____.

Flowers with seeds help to _____.

sunlight
stand up
make more flowers
water
food

All right answers, color in the smile!!

TEACHER'S TALENT PROJECT: TEACHER'S FLOWER GARDEN

Steps: On a piece of white drawing paper, draw shapes to make your flower garden. Trace shapes with ultra fine Sharpie and color in with crayons or colored pencils. Include in your garden a minimum of six different designed flowers in different sizes on the ground with grass, four flying insects, and four creatures that live on the ground.

Day Eleven: Monday

MARY'S CLASSROOM
KINDERGARTEN

LUNCHTIME NOTES

A new student showed up this morning to class, an adorable boy, very quiet and shy. His name is Kevin. This morning we did some artwork and drew our families during class. I went around the room and talked to each student about their drawing. I asked them to explain to me what was happening in their drawing. At this age, when students draw their families or a figure, there is a variety of expressions.

FIGURE 11-1

Some students in my class drew their figures using ovals, triangles, squares, and circles for body, head, legs, arms, and clothing. These figure shapes were repeated throughout their artwork. When drawing key facial characteristics, students also included details such as houses, birds, eyeglasses, shoes, a purse, or a bow in the hair.

Colors were used as they appear in nature and as the family stood on the grass (a baseline) there is an exaggeration of sizes between figures as dad and mom were taller than the house. The skyline was drawn at the top of the drawing. Students at this age are drawing what they know based on their concept and not perception of an object.

While moving throughout the room, I observed other students in my class expressed their family and figures with fewer details. A circle was drawn for the head with lines or shapes suggesting arms and legs. Some figures are neither male nor female and added details were distorted and exaggerated. Colors used were not representational and appeared to be more subjective and emotional. Additional objects were floating and randomly placed in the drawing. Based upon my observation of the family drawings, it shows that my kindergarten students have a range of skills and life experiences.

FIGURE 11-2

When I saw Kevin's drawing, it was very different. The major portion of his drawing was filled with many circles with lines radiating from the center. Some images had a circle with four lines drawn from the circle and few lines represented hair and toes.

FIGURE 11-3

Around the edges were intricate loops, swirls, and random lines. It appears that his images were not as developed as the other students in the class. I asked him to tell me about his drawing. He pointed to four circles with lines indicating parents, sister, and him. Additional lines randomly drawn represented pets, while other lines represented trees and birds outside.

I am aware that fine motor skills, muscle development, and visual acuity are influenced by a child's level of physical development and in turn affect child's artistic expression. Also, an art image and its meaning expressed by a child is influenced by emotional makeup, personality, and temperament. What a child perceives is drawn rather than what is realistically presented. When a child creates, he or she is relying on memories, experiences, and images; what a child knows is the subject of the drawing. After school, I will review Lowenfeld's stages of artistic development for children, so I can gain knowledge about Kevin's drawing.

FIGURE 11-4

AFTER SCHOOL READING

Viktor Lowenfeld's *Creative and Mental Growth* (1947), when published, became the main resource for art and classroom educators. Throughout his life, Lowenfeld was involved in the arts: as a musician he played the violin, he was a painter, a visual and performing artist, and throughout his educational career became a lasting influence in the field of Art Education.

Lowenfeld's theory describes the beginning of expression with scribbling, which normally occurs in 1- to 3-year-olds. The Scribbling Stage is broken up into four subcategories: (1) disordered—uncontrolled markings, (2) longitudinal (11-5), (3) controlled repetitions, and (4) circular (11-6 and 11-7). There is no real connection between the marks on the paper and their representation. Lowenfeld stresses that the scribbling stage is an important developmental period for a child, because it is the beginning of self-expression, manipulation, and exploration of tools. The child then proceeds to naming images (11-8).

FIGURE 11-5

FIGURE 11-6

FIGURE 11-7

FIGURE 11-8

The second stage in Lowenfeld's theory is called the <u>Pre-schematic Stage</u> and children are between the ages of 3 and 4. In this stage the children start to make shapes and name the objects of people and pets familiar to them. These figures are sometimes called "tadpole" figures because they have a body with arms and legs sticking out.

When children are 5 or 6 they are in the third, or <u>Schematic, stage</u> (11-9 and 11-10). In this stage children have clearly assigned shapes to objects. They have a schema for creating drawings, there is a defined order, and there is a clear separation between sky and ground. Important objects are often drawn larger than lesser important objects.

FIGURE 11-9

FIGURE 11-10

FIGURE 11-11

FIGURE 11-12

The fourth stage is the <u>Dawning Realism</u> (11-11). Children are 7 to 9 years old and are more critical of their own work. Their schema is more complex and overlapping can be seen. It is apparent that there is a sense of spatial relationships.

Lowenfeld's next stage, the <u>Pseudo-Naturalistic Stage</u> (11-12), includes children between the ages of 10 and 13. Children in this stage use value and light, shading, color combinations, and perspective to add a dimensional effect. The product becomes most important to the artist and can reflect an emotional reaction using color to reflect personal feelings. Or, the artist can be inspired by visual imagery.

CONCLUSION

My students who draw figures using the geometric shapes, including details, decorations, and defining of spatial awareness based on placement of images, are exhibiting Lowenfeld's Schematic Stage of artistic development. Other students in my class, whose figure drawings have little details and are randomly placed on the paper with no relationship, correlate to Lowenfeld Pre-Schematic stages of artistic development. Kevin's art reflects a late Scribbling Stage.

Additional authors who write about the children's art stages include Rhoda Kellogg (1967) who was a psychologist and a nursery school educator, and published an archive of 8,000 drawings by children. A contemporary of Lowenfeld was Jean Piaget, a Swiss psychologist (1972). His theory on developmental stages is known as cognitive development, and explains how children's thinking changes over time due to interactions with people and environments, thereby refining mental constructs. Similar to Piaget's theory was Lev Vygotsky, a Soviet developmental psychologist. His theory differs with emphasis on the role of language and direct instruction in learning that is embedded in a child's family and cultural context. According to the author Eisner (1976), what children know will be expressed in their artistic creations, thus reflecting a relationship between learning, thinking, and art.

UPDATE

I am glad I talked with my Kevin's parents. I explained my concern about his motor skills, how he represents his images, and his difficulties to stay on task in the classroom. They shared with me the difficulties Kevin had with his health since he was a baby. He was not able to be as active as other children, and they appreciated my concerns.

We agreed to work as a team by introducing activities to help improve Kevin's visual perception and motor skills. We will implement hidden picture games such as *Where's Wally,* talk about what we see in famous paintings, and enjoy completing puzzles. To develop strong muscles in Kevin's fingers, hands, and wrists we will use play-dough, crayon coloring, cutting and pasting paper, drawing with a pencil in his ARTBOOK, and painting in his art center at home.

As a motivation for Kevin to complete his schoolwork, we will employ "The Sticker Chart" as a reward system. We agreed to meet again in a month and evaluate these strategies for their effectiveness. I think this approach will enhance Kevin's progress and academic improvement.

Day Twelve: Tuesday

ESTHER'S CLASSROOM
THIRD GRADE

EARLY MORNING NOTES

The science project I am planning to teach is divided into two sections—the classroom's archaeological dig, focusing on fossils; and the Mesozoic era plus dinosaurs. The Science unit will begin with the introduction of the Mesozoic era using YouTube videos, covering the three periods, Triassic, Jurassic, and Cretaceous, and types of dinosaurs. Students will participate in an archaeological dig enriching the concept of a timeline, "As you dig down, you travel back in time" and will recognize the fossil-making process.

Essential Questions

Why is it important to learn about Earth's history?
What information can you gather to support your idea about life in the Mesozoic era?
Can you elaborate on the reason the dinosaurs died out?

Standards

Science: 4DESS1.3 Fossils provide evidence about the plants and animals that lived long ago and the nature of the environment at that time.

National Visual Arts Standards:
- Creating: VA:Cr1.2.3a: Apply knowledge of available resources tools and technologies to investigate personal ideas through the art making process.

- Presenting: VA: Pr6.1.3a: Identify and explain how and where different cultures illustrate stories and history of life through art.

Objectives: The student will:

- Recite the rhyme about the Mesozoic era.
- Illustrate the environment during the Mesozoic era.
- Identify artifacts from different time periods.
- Create a fossil using clay.

Vocabulary

Paleontology is the study of items left behind by living organisms during Earth's history, focusing on the study of fossils.

Archaeology is the study of human activity in the past, primarily through the recovery and analysis of materials.

Fossils are the remains of once living animals or plants, which give us information about how animals and plants lived in the past.

Timeline is usually a visual resource used to display a list of events in chronological order.

Mesozoic Era, called the age of reptiles, included Triassic, Jurassic, and Cretaceous periods covering 186 million years.

OVERVIEW OF MESOZOIC ERA

The Earth was very different during the Mesozoic era: the shape of the continents, the climate, the animals, and the environment. At the beginning of the Mesozoic era, there was a supercontinent called Pangaea, which eventually started to separate toward the middle of the era. At the beginning of the era, coniferous plants already existed and became more abundant. Towards the end of the era, plant life was lush with numerous flowering plants. During this era, monstrous beasts such as giant reptiles and dinosaurs roamed the Earth. Toward the end of the era, 65 million years ago, volcanic eruptions caused an increase in sea surface temperatures, which prevented sea life. Then, the effects of a six-mile-wide asteroid impacted earth, blocked the sun and eventually caused the demise of the dinosaurs. This era spans from about 252 million years ago to about 65 million years ago, and is known as the Age of Reptiles or the Age of Dinosaurs.

The *Triassic Period* began 248 million years ago on the land of Pangaea. The climate was hot and dry, catering to small and fast dinosaurs such as Asylosaurus, Eoraptor, and tiny night mammals. On the land ferns, cycads, and horsetail plants grew.

The *Jurassic period* began 208 million years ago, when Pangaea started to break up into parts. Climate was hot and dry with some flooding. Dinosaurs increased in number including Apatosaurus, Stegosaurus, Sinraptor, and the first primitive dinosaur-like bird developed.

The *Cretaceous period* began 146 million years ago while the continents were drifting further apart with volcanic activity and a warm climate. In the beginning of this period, sea levels were high and toward the end the sea levels dropped with extreme temperatures. Dinosaurs flourished such as Ankylosaurus, Iguanodon, Triceratops, Tyrannosaurus, and Velociraptor. The oldest known ants, snakes, and butterflies arose toward the end of the era, along with flowering plants. When an asteroid hit the earth, the dinosaurs and other prehistoric animals died out, thus ending this period.

Resources

Videos on fossils / Mesozoic era:
> *Denizens of the Mesozoic, Mesozoic Era, The Time of the King, What Is a Fossil?*

Posters of dinosaurs
Timeline of the Mesozoic era
Dinosaur rhyme

Art Materials:

Drawing paper 12" x 18"
Pencils, eraser, oil pastels

Art Language

Spatial positioning is foreground, middleground, and background.
Shapes in the foreground are larger and are smaller in the background.
Pattern is the repetition of shapes, colors, and lines.

SCIENCE PROJECT PART 1

Students will view the videos on the Mesozoic era, discuss the three periods and their characteristics. The rhyme is introduced to the students.

Dinosaur Art Project:

1. Students define space by drawing the background with the volcanoes; the middleground with land; and the foreground with large dinosaurs.
2. Shapes of the animals are drawn with pencil.
3. The animals are colored in with oil pastels.
4. The shapes are then outlined with a black oil pastel. (12-1)

Dinosaurs lived a long time ago
In the Mes-o-zo-ic era
Don't you know.
This era is divided into three,
Now you'll say it, say it with me.
Tri-as-sic,
Jur as-sic and
Cre-ta-ceous Per-iod.

FIGURE 12-1

OVERVIEW ABOUT FOSSILS

FIGURE 12-2

Studying fossils, which are the remains of ancient animals and plants from past geologic ages on Earth, tell us the story of sea creatures and animals. Two hundred million years ago, the animals and plants on Pangaea left remains, making it possible for us today to find fossils on every continent.

FIGURE 12-3

The experience of participating in an archaeological dig, whether it is in the classroom or out in the field, has fashioned and inspired many future scientific careers in our young students. As students in the classroom dig dirt and shake their screens, to uncover their find, they will record their discovery on the Recording Sheet referencing a timeline display.

Art Materials:

Clay, kiln, acrylic paint
Items to press into the clay: plastic leaves
Plastic dinosaurs from the dollar store (12-2)
Fossil molds from school specialty store (12-3)
Shells

Art Language

Texture is the visual and tactile quality of a surface—that is, how the surface feels. *Relief* refers to sections of a surface that are raised above the rest of the material.

FOSSIL ART PROJECT

1. Students receive a lump of clay and flatten it, no higher than 2 inches.
2. Students make multiple impressions in the clay using plastic dinosaur feet, fossil molds, plastic leaves, and shells (12-4).
3. After the clay has dried, it is fired in the kiln.
4. Students, using a sponge with acrylic paint, cover the surface of the clay fossil (12-5, 12-6).

Assessment

Dinosaur Art Project:
1. Students recite the Mesozoic era rhyme.
2. Finished artwork depicts animals and environment during the Mesozoic era.

Fossils Art Project:
1. Clay fossil is completed.
2. Student fills in worksheet for the archaeological dig.

Fossils were made in the past millions of years ago.
Of sea creatures and dinosaurs that died from what we know.
Let me dig and discover treasures from earth's history,
And uncover fossils that might solve a mystery.

FIGURE 12-4   FIGURE 12-5

FIGURE 12-6

SCIENCE PROJECT PART 2
I'm Digging It – An Archaeological Dig

Students will view the *Fossils* video and how they are made. The rhyme will be introduced to the students. The teacher will demonstrate how students will work the dig and record their findings. Two or three students will work as a team and sign up to reserve a time slot to work on the dig.

SETTING UP A CLASSROOM ARCHAEOLOGICAL DIG
Materials:

Plastic sheet for the floor
2 X-large garbage bags
2 X-large containers
Potting soil, 2 dirt scoopers
Two screens used to sift the soil
Layer 4: Collection of authentic fossils
Layer 3: Pottery shards with geometric designs
Layer 2: Revolutionary War artifacts
Layer 1: Parts from an electronic item
Recorder Worksheet
Display board with labeled artifact images found in each layer

Setting up a Dig:

1. Place the large sheets of plastic on the floor under two extra large containers.
2. The best containers are the large plastic tubs that you find at Walmart.
3. Place inside each container an extra large garbage bag.
4. Make two soil sifters by stapling a screen onto old frames or constructed wooden squares.
5. Collect authentic fossils and war artifacts by attending a mineral show.
6. Pottery Shards: Smash an old piece of pottery with designs or draw on a slab of clay geometric patterns with a black marker. Then break the clay up into pieces making sure there are no sharp points.
7. Collect present-day electronic items such as floppy disk, CD, mouse, wires, any small items from a computer, phone, or play station.
8. In one large container, place soil in the bottom, add Layer 4 with fossils, then continue adding soil layers and items till filled.
9. After students scoop the soil onto the sifter, they move over to the empty container and gently shake the sifter to discover their finds. This soil is then used to reset for another original dig.
10. As students uncover items, they record their findings on their worksheet using the display board as reference.
11. When the students have completed their dig, the teacher will reset the dirt and item layers for the next set of students to dig up.
12. The display board designed by the teacher is based upon collected items for the dig.

COMMENTS FROM THE AUTHOR

When I was an elementary art teacher, Archaeology and Paleontology was one of the favorite-teaching units I taught to my students. Needless to say, they found this unit intriguing and exciting, not only participating in the archaeological dig that I set up in the room, but also doing research on dinosaurs and fossils. The media specialist in the library complained about the demand by students for books and videos on these topics, because her resources were completely depleted.

Resetting the container for the dig was demanding; however, the looks of enthusiasm and enjoyment from the students was well worth all of the energy used to collect the items and keep the dig up-to-date in the room. If you decide to implement a classroom archaeology dig, you will not regret it. I know, because I can still remember the smiles on my students' faces after all these years.
J. Wachtman

TIMELINE BOARD ON ARTIFACTS

Level 1   2000s Present Time   Photograph of Items

Electronics pieces
CD
Floppy disk
Mouse
Flash drive
Computer Cables/Wires

Level 2   1700s Revolutionary War

Musket ball
Part of the Flag
Buttons
Coins
Piece of Declaration
Fabric

Level 3   15,000 Years Ago American Indian

Pottery Shard
Arrowheads
Basket Reed
Stone Tools

Level 4   348 Million Years Ago

Fossils
Ammonites
Leaves
Trilobites
Shells
Fish

DIGGING IT, AN ARCHAEOLOGICAL DIG

Recording Worksheet
Record your finds by either writing the name of the item or
drawing the item in the correct layer.

Names: _____

Layer 1 Write the Historic Time:_____

Layer 2 Write the Historic Time:_____

Layer 3 Write the Historic Time:_____

Layer 4 Write the Historic Time:_____

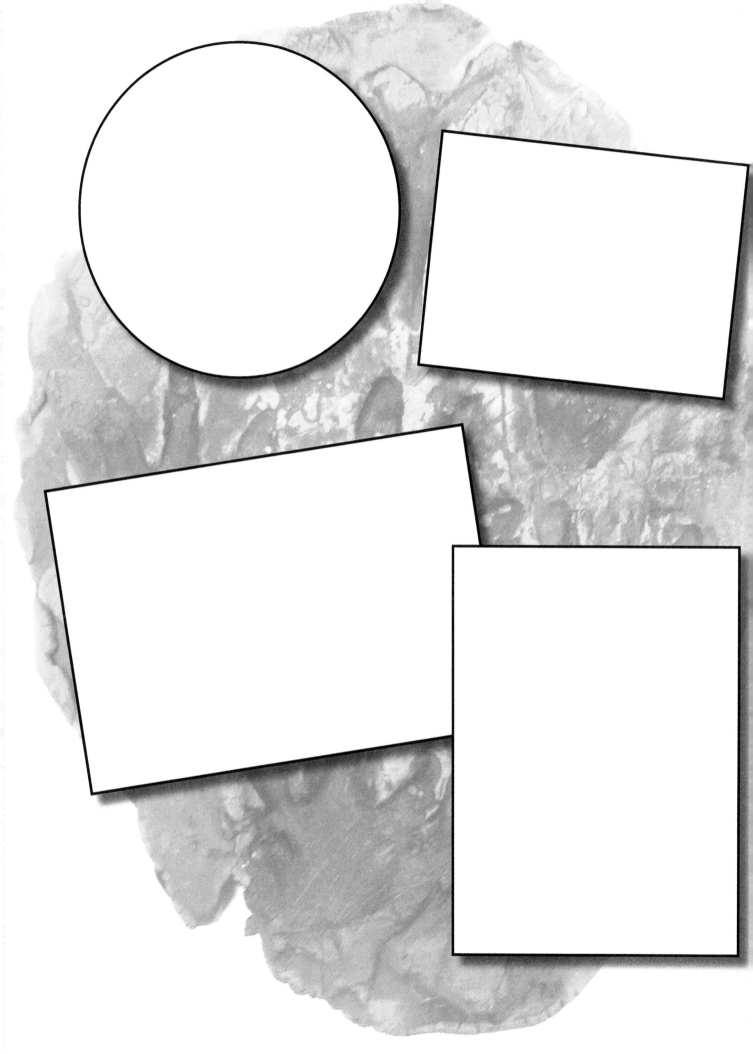

Day Thirteen: Wednesday

SHARLENE'S ART ROOM

AFTER FACULTY WORKSHOP

I think it was an informative workshop for the teachers! This workshop on *How To Talk About Art* will help teachers to enhance their lessons. Teachers appreciate the importance of enriching their lessons by incorporating a visual image such as an art poster, book illustration, or an Internet slide related to the subject being taught. The handout presented to teachers in today's art workshop describes strategies to implement art concepts and projects in their classroom lessons.

HANDOUT FOR TEACHERS
How to Talk About Art: Art Criticism

When students interact with the teacher in a discussion about the artwork, the teacher is creating a stimulating environment that initiates the building blocks for thinking and understanding. Art criticism contains four components: describe, analyze, interpret, and judge. When using art visuals as part of a classroom lesson and applying the art criticism format, asking the following questions will attract students' attention and engage their minds.

The purpose of asking art criticism questions is to help students appreciate and understand the meaning of a work of art. When students talk and write about art, inquire and question, they are thinking, feeling, and voicing personal opinions that are neither right nor wrong. Thus, students are scratching below the surface to discover, appreciate, and enjoy artistic creations.

DESCRIBE

When a teacher introduces a visual during a lesson, they can ask this question, *As you look at the art, what images do you recognize?* Students respond by voicing their opinion or they can write a list. Students are identifying the content or subject matter of the art, and are engaging in the exercise of perception and memory.

ANALYZE

Instead of asking students, "What elements and principles of art do you see in the art work?" use this questioning technique: *What colors did the artist use most? What is special about the colors? Do you see any geometric or free-form shapes, and if so where are they located in the art? Is the artist depicting a two-dimensional or a three-dimensional effect? What is the most important image in the art? Are there patterns in the art? What kind of texture is implied?*

INTERPRET

What's happening in the picture? What's the story? What does the picture seem to be saying? These questions will inspire, stimulate, and evoke imagination in students as they formulate their thoughts. As students share their idea of the story, this experience becomes a memorable and relevant activity. The teacher can enhance their learning experience by adding to the story, and providing additional details about the artist or the time the artwork depicts.

As students respond to questions, it is important to continue the dialogue by saying, *What do you see that tells you that?* Based on the student's culture and childhood experiences, some answers might surprise you. A student once stated, "Romare Bearden was a very poor artist." When asked *What makes you say that?* the response was, "because he had only newspaper to make his art."

JUDGE

Judging a work of art is evaluating its artistic merit. Include some of these questions when talking about art. *What do you think of this artwork? How do you rate the artist's craftsmanship (1-10, 10 is highest)? Is the artwork successful in expressing the theme, subject, or idea portrayed in the art?*

What degree of imagination has the artist displayed in the artwork? Did the artist successfully depict a specific art style—Realism, Abstraction, Expressionism, Fantasy, or Non-Objective?

Aesthetics is more than thinking about the ideas behind the art, it is about feelings. While in the classroom, listen for students making comments about items or images in the room, such as *That's ugly!* or *That's my favorite picture!* Take the opportunity to initiate a discussion with, *What makes you say that? What don't you like about this image?*

When a discussion about the artwork implicates a social, political, religious, economic, or philosophical influence, this approach is called Contextualism. Ask the question, *What do you think was going on in the world at this time?* This perspective lends itself to the study of Social Studies and History.

Referencing art knowledge, the teacher can ask questions emphasizing the elements and principles of art, the art materials, technique, and style. This approach is referred to as Formalism, where the focus is on the art itself, materials used, craftsmanship, and originality.

Students need time and opportunity to explain their thoughts; therefore, provide a platform and involve other students in the discussion by asking, *Who agrees with this comment?*

Review of Components of Art Criticism:

- <u>Describe</u> what you see in the art.
- <u>Analyze</u> the elements and principles of art.
- <u>Interpret</u> the artwork. What's the story?
- <u>Judge</u> the artist's skill and intention in the work.

Answer the following questions as you view the painting (13-1).

Art Criticism Questions

- Describe what you see in the painting.

- State the art style of this painting and its characteristics.

- Create a story about this painting.

- What are the dominant elements and principles of art in the artwork?

- How do you rate the artist's art skill?

- How does this art make you feel?

- Additional Comments:

FIGURE 13-1

NOTES

DEFINITIONS
The Elements and Principles of Art

Line: The path of a moving dot through space and has more length than thickness. Lines can be vertical, horizontal, diagonal, zigzag, curved, or spiral.

Shape: A two-dimensional area with identifiable boundaries, which uses an enclosed line to create geometric and free-form shapes, such as a circle, square, rectangle, oval, triangle, and organic.

Form: A three-dimensional area with identifiable boundaries such as a sphere, cube, pyramid, cylinder, and organic.

Color: What the eye sees when light is viewed directly or as reflected light. Daylight contains light waves of all colors. Characteristics of color are hue, value warm and cool, intensity, primary, secondary, complementary, intermediate, neutral, tint, and shade.

Texture: Refers to surface quality and the way things look or feel. Textures can be smooth, rough, jagged, soft, hard, or implied.

Space: Actual open air around a sculpture or work of architecture. A form occupies space and has three-dimensional characteristics of height, width, and depth. On a 2-D surface certain techniques can create the illusion of space by using:

- Overlapping of shapes
- Sizes of shapes being larger in foreground and smaller in background
- Positioning of images in foreground, middleground, and background
- Colors—warm colors advance while cool colors recede
- Linear Perspective uses a scientific approach that parallel lines recede to a vanishing point

Value: The relative lightness or darkness of a color, which creates contrast and interest in the artwork.

Principles of Art

Pattern: The repetition of an element of art such as lines, colors, and shapes in artwork.

Balance: The equilibrium of various elements in a work of art:
Symmetrical: A mirror image creating a visual balance.
Asymmetrical: Two sides that do not correspond to one another in size, shape, and placement, creating a feeling balance.
Radial Balance: The design initiates at the center and can be divided into two identical halves

Emphasis: The center of interest, the focal point.

Variety: Includes differences in scale, surface, line, value, and shape that give interest and contrast to a composition.

Proportion: The pleasing relationship of all parts to each other and to the whole of the design.

Unity: The sense of oneness, of things belonging together and making up a coherent whole.

What are the Dominant Elements and Principles of Art

FIGURE 13-2

You Can Identify in Each of the Following Works of Art?

#1

Elements:

Principles:

FIGURE 13-3

#2

Elements:

Principles:

FIGURE 13-4

#3

Elements:

Principles:

NOTES

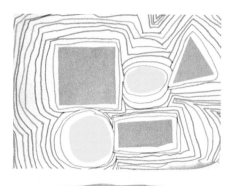

#4

Elements:

Principles:

FIGURE 13-5

#5

Elements:

Principles:

FIGURE 13-6

#6

Elements:

Principles:

FIGURE 13-7

#7

Elements:

Principles:

FIGURE 13-8

#8

Elements:

Principles:

#9

Elements:

Principles

FIGURE 13-11

#10

Elements:

Principles:

ART FOR THE ELEMENTARY EDUCATOR

Day Fourteen: Thursday

JEROME'S CLASSROOM
SECOND GRADE

EARLY MORNING NOTES

On the way to school today, I was trying to decide how to make today's writing lesson more interesting and personal for my students. I went to the art room and checked with Sharlene, asking her for ideas for an art activity to complement our writing activity for later today. Sharlene went through her files and gave me a CD, which contained a PowerPoint presentation on the artist, Faith Ringgold, and a quilt-making art activity. This afternoon, I will explain to students the use of quilts in history, and introduce Faith Ringgold's painted story quilts as motivation for the art project and writing lesson. I will format the lesson during lunchtime.

QUILT RHYME

Quilts can tell a story
of heroes and glory.
A life event and many
celebrations spent.
A personal story
in a quilt,
shows family history
being built.

LANGUAGE ARTS LESSON
Essential Questions:

Why are stories so appealing? Can you recall an event in your life that you could place on a quilt?

Objectives: The student will:

- Define the following: Quilt and Story Quilt.
- Realize that quilts can be objects of both everyday use and art.
- Make a quilt square and write a personal story.

Standards

- CCSS.ELA-LITERACY.L.2.2
- Demonstrate command of the conventions of Standard English capitalization, punctuation, and spelling when writing.
- Creating: VA: Cr1.2.2a: Make art or design with various materials and tools to explore personal interests, questions and curiosity.
- Connecting: VA: Cn10.1.2a: Create works of art about events in home school or community life.

Art Materials:

Large color construction paper 18" x18"
White drawing paper 5" x 5"
Pencil, eraser, crayons, yarn
Precut paper squares with various patterns
Story Quilts, a PowerPoint presentation illustrating the history of quilt making (Retrieved April 1, 2015 http://helenrindsberg.myiglou.com/StudioCourse/FAQ00015.htm)
CD - a PowerPoint presentation on Faith Ringgold's art

Art Language

A *quilt* is a cloth sandwich, with a top, which is usually the decorated part, a back, and filler in the middle.
A *story* is a narrative that can be true or fictitious, in prose or verse, designed to interest, amuse, or instruct the listener or reader.
Pattern is the repetition of shapes or colors.

Introduction

Students are introduced to quilt making; it is like a cloth sandwich using familiar scraps of material, decorated and the inside is stuffed with filler. Quilts can be considered a work of art; they can also tell stories through pictures about the people who made them and record traditions, personal events, and folktales. Some segments of the *History of Quilts,* an online PowerPoint presentation, are introduced to the students. Students discuss the different uses of quilts throughout history and how they can be objects of both everyday use and art. A brief description of Faith Ringgold's story is told to the students, and then they view the CD presentation on her story quilts. After the students make comments

FIGURE 14-1

Appliquéd Fabric representing life in the Peruvian mountains.

FIGURE 14-2

Writing on Artwork: I'm ice-skating. I was skating in the afternoon. I ice skated because I wanted to learn how too. I'm skating in a skating rink.

about her artwork, the teacher inquires, "*Students do you want to share something about yourself that could be placed in a quilt square?*"

Background Information

Faith Ringgold is an African-American artist and author known for her painted story quilts, in which she combines painting, quilted fabric, and storytelling. Ringgold's artworks contain simple, bold, large shapes, with shining colors. As a child, her great-great-grandmother showed her how to make quilts, as it was their tradition. Quilts serve various purposes such as providing warmth, preserving memories, recording events, and storytelling. Ringgold used her art to tell her own story resulting in her first "story" quilt called, *Who's Afraid of Aunt Jemima?*

She also began to write stories for children, such as *Tar Beach*, which told the story of her childhood in Harlem. A publisher who saw this art suggested that she tell the story in a book, along with her illustrations. After this successful writ-

FIGURE 14-3

NOTES

Writing on Artwork: I wanted to save the world. I was in space on my birthday. There was an asteroid. It was heading towards earth. It hit my Space ship and broke it in half.

ing, she authored numerous children's books. Famous artists such as Matisse and Picasso impacted some images in her story quilts. Also, Ringgold, by drawing their stories, celebrated different cultures in a mural for a community.

Art Project:

1. Students draw and color themselves on the 5" x 5" white drawing paper.
2. The drawing, with a colored pattern design, is then glued in the center of a larger square of colored construction paper. This paper is then glued to a larger, 18" x 18" colored paper.
3. Squares made from material are precut and glued around the art creating a border.
4. Holes are punched around the edge of the large colored construction paper, with yarn woven in and out of the holes.
5. Students write their sentences around the artwork,

Language Arts Assessment:

1. Students, within a discussion, explain the difference between a quilt and story quilt, and describe its various uses.

FIGURE 14-4

Writing on Artwork: One day it started to snow. I had just gotten some new ice skates. I went outside and started to ice skate. I had lots of fun.

ART FOR THE ELEMENTARY EDUCATOR

2. Students write complete sentences using capitalization, punctuation, and spelling.

Visual Arts Assessment:

Quilt square completed by following all of the art steps.

Instructional Strategies

It's the goal of every teacher to celebrate student success in the learning process. Marsha Tate is a well-known lecturer and educational consultant and has taught over 125,000 administrators, teachers, parents, and business and community leaders throughout the world. Tate (2003b) wrote and published *Worksheets Don't Grow Dendrites: 20 Instructional Strategies that Engage the Brain.* She presents the latest research in brain-based learning and how instructional strategies can motivate learners and increase understanding and long-term retention.

This lesson, *Story Quilts,* contains four instructional strategies—storytelling, artwork, writing, and rhyme. As students listen to a story, they focus on the storyline, the brain relaxes and the mind visualizes mental images as the story progresses. This activity of storytelling and visualization enhances students' learning and recalling of information. The strategy of art making supports students' learning by enhancing the visual-spatial intelligence. When students are in the creative process of making art, this activity generates an emotionally charged memory, which increases their retention of content.

When a student records information, the brain remembers this material because of the activity of processing, retaining, and retrieving the information. When students engage in writing activities in all disciplines, their skills improve, thus enhancing their long-term memory, awareness of patterns, and enriching conceptual development.

The brain responds to rhythmic patterns. The strategy of rhyming assists students in connecting content together and increases a meaningful learning experience to memory. This strategy also helps students to develop precise phonemic awareness skills—a critical early reading skill that gives students a strong foundation for beginning reading.

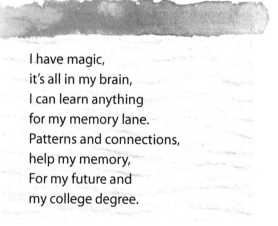

I have magic,
it's all in my brain,
I can learn anything
for my memory lane.
Patterns and connections,
help my memory,
For my future and
my college degree.

This skill is accomplished because students are engaged in isolating, blending, and manipulating sounds on several levels.

Tate's *20 Instructional Strategies*, when merged within lessons, enables the teacher to provide an environment with an atmosphere that is friendly, inspiring, thought provoking, and encouraging.
Following is the list of strategies formulated by Tate (2003a).

Tate's *20 Instructional Strategies That Engage the Brain*

Strategy 1 Brainstorming and Discussion
Strategy 2 Drawing and Artwork
Strategy 3 Field Trips
Strategy 4 Games
Strategy 5 Graphic Organizers, Semantic Maps, and Word Webs
Strategy 6 Humor
Strategy 7 Manipulatives, Experiments, Labs, and Models
Strategy 8 Metaphors, Analogies, and Similes
Strategy 9 Mnemonic Devices
Strategy 10 Movement
Strategy 11 Music, Rhythm, Rhyme, and Rap
Strategy 12 Project-Based and Problem-Based Instruction
Strategy 13 Reciprocal Teaching and Cooperative Learning
Strategy 14 Role Plays, Drama, Pantomimes, and Charades
Strategy 15 Storytelling
Strategy 16 Technology
Strategy 17 Visualization and Guided Imagery
Strategy 18 Visuals
Strategy 19 Work Study and Apprenticeships
Strategy 20 Writing and Journals

Day Fifteen: Friday

ESTHER'S CLASSROOM
THIRD GRADE

MORNING NOTES, BEFORE THE BELL RINGS

TGIF…It was a long week. The newest email from the principal asks us to review our room's learning centers, and how they support student learning. She attended the *Annual Teacher's Conference,* in San Antonio, Texas, and was impressed with a presentation on the value of learning centers reaching all learning types and specifically addressing Gardner's "Multiple Intelligences." The attached material is from the conference. She would like us to review the contents and consider any improvements or modifications to our classroom's learning centers.

CLASSROOM LEARNING CENTERS—
Supporting Multiple Intelligences

A learning center is a space set aside in the classroom. It provides students with a variety of materials and opportunities to enrich and enhance their knowledge. There are a few considerations for setting up centers: the size of the classroom, the amount of space available for one or more centers, furniture, and materials needs.

The primary concern for centers is to address students' interests and educational needs. Typically, learning centers in the classroom focused on "enrichment," which included art and reading activities. Presently, neuroscience research is explaining how the brain learns, and assessment in education stresses performance-based activities. In view of this knowledge, the learning center has become a valuable, integral asset in the classroom. Centers can be designed to support discipline standards by reinforcing skills such as reading or math; and exploratory centers can engage various learning styles and intelligences, giving students the ability, based on their interest, to choose a center's activity. Students can explore, discover, learn, and express delight with themselves by taking charge of their learning.

A teacher's goal is to provide a flourishing and encouraging learning environment for students and this includes learning centers. A key for designing effective learning centers is applying organizational skills. This can be achieved by correlating a center's activity with materials in conjunction to the lesson's content being taught in the classroom. The examination of curriculum topics in the areas of Science, Social Studies, Math, and Language Arts can produce a list of possible themes for developing learning centers.

Themes in Science can include outer space, weather, life in the ocean, and fossils. Topics such as geography, biographies of famous figures, and cultures are taught in Social Studies classes. Math themes include symmetry, time, graphs, charts, geometry, and patterns. Language Arts embrace poetry, grammar, folktales, storytelling, reading, and creative writing.

Another key for designing effective learning centers is conducting research that links Gardner's Multiple Intelligences (MI) with the learning center's activities and materials. Howard Gardner, a psychologist and professor of neuroscience from Harvard University, first published *Frames of Mind* in 1983, which identified seven distinct intelligences. Upon revision of his theory, Gardner added an eighth intelligence, Naturalist, and has suggested there are a few more. "MI theory" research indicates that an individual has the ability to perform a number of independent intelligences such as Linguistic, Spatial, Logical, and Musical.

Even though each individual possesses a range of intelligences, an individual can demonstrate greater knowledge or strength in a specific intelligence. This strength does not indicate strength or weakness in any other intelligence, because no two individuals have the same configuration (Gardner, 1991). Students learn, understand, and express their knowledge in a variety of ways (intelligences), and to address those needs it is important for educators to present content by implementing a range of teaching strategies. Learning materials and activities designed for centers need to be interesting, stimulating, and challenging for the student. Technology use in learning centers motivates and entices students to participate in activities. It is important to select the appropriate multimedia for a specific learning modality. The following content provides ideas and suggestions for developing learning centers that merge with Multiple Intelligences for the classroom.

Supplies in *Center One* include art tools such as markers, crayons, watercolor paints with brushes, and modeling clay that supports motor skills. Included in the center are earphones plugged into a programed MP3 player. This allows stu-

NOTES

dents to listen and move to music while creating. The center contains Music Activity Cards suggesting students paint a picture inspired by the music, or after completing a drawing, write a song to accompany it. In addition, this allows students to combine movement to their song. Sharing this creative process and product with the class enhances the student's confidence and self-esteem.

Students share their projects with the class, because the teacher has scheduled and set aside time during the school year for the *Center Time Presentations.* The teacher makes available an inexpensive digital camera for students to check out. As students snap photographs, their visual perception is enhanced as the user looks through the camera's viewfinder, composes, and focuses on a specific object. A computer is available for students to download photographs and produce a presentation using a slide show or PowerPoint as their classroom project. These center activities can be interrelated to subjects being taught, and involve the Visual/Spatial, Musical, and Kinesthetic learners.

Materials in *Center Two* include books of poetry and stories that students can be read into a recorder. A number of blank journals are used for students to write creative narratives or poetry. Word games can be challenging and a computer can provide a foreign language for students to learn. Bookmarked computer sites can support the teacher's Language Arts lesson, allowing students to engage in specific writings or listen to stories. Students can initiate a monthly classroom newsletter using interviews of fellow students asking questions, and opinions to specific topics. This center speaks to the Linguistic learners.

Center Three contains materials that employ the qualities of logic. Students seek activities that solve problems, such as mathematical calculations, unraveling a mystery, and analyzing and categorizing facts and information. The center includes a microscope with slides. Students view slides of various items such as insects, plants, rock, mineral, fibers, and animal parts such as hair and scales. Students record their observations, and collect data and share this project via computer to the class. This center is for students who display aptitude for numbers, detecting patterns and logical thinking; solving brainteasers, games, puzzles, and riddles, and creating strategy games.

Center Four accommodates the students who are sensitive to other people, have an outgoing personality, and flourish in a cooperative setting with other students. These students demonstrate leadership qualities in the classroom debate or perform in a government role. Tutoring or mentoring students in the classroom exemplifies the social skills of this personality. The Interpersonal Intelligence students as facilitators use this center as a meeting place for group projects related to educational issues taught and approved by the teacher.

Center Five is designed for independent learners who are motivated and aware of their feelings, moods, and goals. Items in this center contain writing materials with suggested projects, such as interpreting a work of art, reflecting and describing personal values, explaining personal philosophy, and listing weekly goals. These Intrapersonal Intelligence students conduct research based upon their interests, designing and creating accompanying images or models.

Center Six might look like a small forest, because Naturalistic Intelligence students love the outdoors, animals, and plants. All students in the classroom will be able to view flower seeds sprouting, feed the rabbit in the cage, identify rocks in a display box using a chart, and examine leaves and insects preserved in containers. Center tools include microscopes, magnifying lenses, and drawing materials for close observations and recording data. A computer is used for researching the habitat and characteristics of an animal that is displayed with its image and research information. The Naturalistic Intelligence students bring their nature experiences into the classroom. They like to share with their classmates a video about their camping trip or exhibit either their photographs from their nature walk or their art drawings inspired by nature. Drawing outside is called *Plein Air*, a French term meaning "in the open air."

Knowing the Intelligence strengths of students in their classroom will aid the teacher in the planning of learning centers, materials, and activities. Information and resources can be found on the website *Multiple Intelligence Survey for Kids,* by Laura Chandler, at http://www.lauracandler.com/free/misurvey.

On this site is a link (http://www.literacynet.org/mi/assessment/findyourstrengths.html) that contains a free questionnaire assisting in the identification of student intelligence. Once information is revealed and grouped, the teacher can plan the types of learning centers and activities that harmonize with classroom discipline themes throughout the school year.

Learning center activities can enhance students with strong intelligences but also can expose students to the intelligence, which they need to enhance. Learning centers are a valuable educational extension in the classroom, providing a motivating environment for students.

Day Sixteen: Monday

LYNN'S CLASSROOM
FIFTH GRADE

AFTER SCHOOL NOTES

I'm beginning to feel overwhelmed. I have two immediate assignments required for my Masters course. My first assignment examines teaching children with special needs. My second assignment is researching and writing my Master's Project on Personality Styles.

I found two interesting articles on teaching children with special needs. The first article, "Assumptions, Expectations, and Surprises: Teaching Autistic Children Art," is about a middle school art teacher who confronted a teaching challenge. She was assigned to teach art to a class of autistic children. The second article addresses teaching strategies, "Art and Disabilities in the Elementary Classroom."

Assumptions, Expectations, and Surprises: Teaching Autistic Children Art
Author: Mary Adamski-Partow

It was my second year of teaching art at my middle school when I found out that I would have the entire ESE class join my eighth-grade pottery class for the spring semester.

Despite numerous classes dedicated to preparing me for the inclusion of special needs students in my class, I had never had more than one or two students with special needs integrated into my art classes. This would be a challenge to create meaningful activities for the ESE class, while presenting the general education students with the regular curriculum.

Day One—Learning to Do Two Things at Once!

Six students with varying degrees of Autism walked in with twenty-eight other students. I decided to group the students with autism at the same table so that if they needed more extensive instruction I could work with them all as a group. A teacher's aide accompanied two of the students as per their IEP.

My introduction worked fine and as luck would have it, the general education students began the project with very few questions, thus allowing me to spend the rest of the class with the autistic students. Their abilities ran the gamut of the autistic scale. While each student was socially reserved, they varied greatly in their ability to manipulate clay.

The aide and I quickly divided the group into two—those who exhibited great skill in manipulating the clay and those who would need hand-over-hand assistance. The aide would work with the students requiring the most assistance and I would help those who could follow larger "chunks" of instruction.

Later in the Semester—Falling Apart

What happened next, over several weeks of clay class, surprised me. The more advanced group had no difficulty in observing my demonstrations, listening to repeated instructions, and then creating the clay projects along with the general education students. In fact, one autistic student in the advanced group, "Kevin," began to show some talent in working with clay that his work was far superior to most other students' work. This "savant"-like quality was not the thing that surprised me, as I had seen many autistic children show remarkable talent in art.

The surprise was that another of the advanced students, "Bob," began to produce work, which got worse as the semester continued on. "Bob" would speed through the day's lesson, making the projects with little or no care. His work lacked detail and precision.

In addition, he grew impatient with the pace of the class, constantly asking when the piece would be out of the kiln and what would be our next project. My frustration grew in proportion to the speed at which "Bob" would crank out unsatisfactory work. How could I teach my general education students, supply hand-over-hand instruction to the students with very little motor skills, and keep "Bob" engaged? I was beginning to feel overwhelmed and incapable of keeping the class functioning!

ART FOR THE ELEMENTARY EDUCATOR

Even Later in the Semester—Getting My Act Together

A few teaching strategies saved me. First, I asked one of my general education students to work with the students who needed hand-over-hand instruction. They were thrilled to be a teacher's assistant. Next, I videotaped several of the next demos so they could be shown to the entire class while I helped each student.

Finally, I asked "Bob" to just work on anything he wanted when he finished his project. "Free clay time," I called it. He could make whatever he wanted. I figured that would give me a break from his constant requests for more projects to do. I actually worried that he would be at a loss to make things on his own. What happened next surprised the entire ESE staff and me.

Success!! "Bob" began making miniature figurines. They were extraordinary in their detail and texture. He began with animals, particularly dinosaurs (16-1 to 16-3).

FIGURE 16-1

They were perfect tiny reproductions of what one might see in a natural history museum. I asked "Bob" if he was looking at a picture of the animals when he made the figurines. He said that he just remembered what they looked like from seeing a picture a while ago.

FIGURE 16-2

At one point, as the winter holidays approached, Bob presented me with a sculpted manger scene, complete with the three Wisemen, Mary & Joseph, and Baby Jesus. The entire sculpture fit on top of a quarter. "I put a smile on the Baby Jesus," exclaimed a proud "Bob" as he gently bestowed to me his gift. I needed my reading glasses and a magnifying glass to even see the baby Jesus, but each element of the sculpture was remarkably in proportion and executed in amazing detail!

FIGURE 16-3

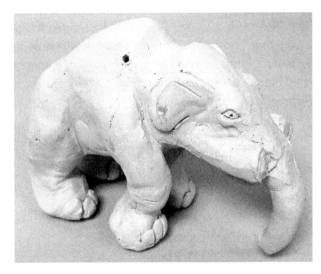

Next came penguin sculptures, hundreds, and the size of grains of rice. "Bob's" talent for imitating life in miniature began to spread through the school, catching the attention of both students and teachers alike.

His other teachers were amazed. Even the student editors of the school's yearbook took notice and planned to do a special page about him. His enthusiasm for his newfound talent began to take on a life of its own. His talent seemed endless; he could sculpt real or imaginary creatures, video game characters, or comic book characters. If he ever saw a picture of it, he could sculpt it! (16-4 to 16-7).

FIGURE 16-4

After consulting with his classroom teachers, we put a plan in place to channel "Bob's" talent into more vocational endeavors. We asked him to create pendants for charms to be used for bracelets and necklaces. Currently, plans are underway to create commercial outlets for "Bob's" creations, and who knows—a possible

ART FOR THE ELEMENTARY EDUCATOR

FIGURE 16-5

FIGURE 16-6

FIGURE 16-7

career in model making. I was also able to use "Bob's" own figurines as quality examples for how he should complete his school projects. As a result, his classroom work improved significantly.

All told, the secret life of the autistic student can seem elusive to teachers. It will always be a challenge to discover that hidden talent, that amazing ability which sets them apart. As teachers, we can so easily fall into the trap of being "the sage on the stage," but with open eyes and a determined effort to keep the curriculum flexible enough we can learn so much!

Art and Disabilities in the Elementary Classroom

Author: Dr. Rick Garner

Inclusion of elementary students with disabilities in art activities is not unlike adapting art activities for any other student. The primary difference is that an adaptation you used in kindergarten for a student without disabilities may also be appropriate for a student with disabilities in the fifth grade. Making these decisions appropriately can be aided by the use of Functional Inventory Measures (FIM), also known as FIM scales.

A FIM scale helps the teacher understand the level of assistance a student may need to perform a given task. Generally, they list a range of functional dimensions such as cognitive, motor, verbal, social, etc. These functions are ranked by the teacher based on how much assistance a student needs with a given functional skill. These levels of assistance can be rated as completely independent (no assistance), minimal assistance, moderate assistance, or maximum assistance.

In the case of art activities, someone who required maximum assistance with motor skills to complete a project may require the commonly used technique of "hand-over-hand." This simply means the teacher or assistant would position a hand on the hand of the student and guide the student in completing the required motor movement (16-8). Activities in art require gross or fine motor control in varying combinations.

A student who requires maximum assistance with gross motor skills might require no assistance with fine motor movement, and vice versa. Stencils are another effective way to ameliorate motor control issues. Cost-effective stencils can be created

FIGURE 16-8

Contributed by Rick Garner. Copyright © Kendall Hunt Publishing Company.

from heavy cardboard acquired for free at any local store that has boxes to discard. Again, the problem here becomes when to use a stencil versus not using a stencil.

A young student with developing motor control needs practice to refine controlled movements and a stencil may inhibit this natural process thereby making the student dependent on a stencil. Making these types of decisions will be an important part of conducting any art activity for students with disabilities.

Most elementary teachers will be working with students who have varying degrees of intellectual disabilities ranging from mild to moderate. One common mistake that teachers make when doing art activities with these students involves giving choices. When giving choices during an art activity it is important to consider the amount of cognitive load you are placing on the student with an intellectual disability. Offering five or six different colored markers to this student can create an overwhelming and ineffective decision-making process that consumes valuable time from the art activity. A simple adjustment to utilizing a binary choice such as, "Do you want red or blue?" can solve this problem and create a much more successful art activity for teacher and student alike. Whereas this seems simple enough, in a room full of young artists franticly creating, it can be easily forgotten.

Another important consideration related to intellectual disabilities involves creating from memory versus drawing from an example or model. Art activities are meant to inspire creativity, but that creativity may be hampered without some basic building blocks.

In art, one of those basic building blocks is visual memory, or the ability to picture objects in one's mind. Without this ability students can experience significant frustration and poor performance on an art task. Thus, students need opportunities to build a repository of mental imagery that will in the future inspire their creative processes. Tracing and copying of a model may be appropriate parts of an art activity for students experiencing mental imagery–related issues in the elementary classroom. As with stencils, however, some students will have a tendency to become dependent on these types of aids, so the teacher must be cautious in making these decisions. A combination of variety and repetition in your intervention choices may best solve any potential dependency problems by alternating the use of such aids throughout an art activity.

Finally, performing a task analysis of a given art activity can assist the elementary teacher in making decisions about the amount and types of assistance students may need to be successful artists in their classroom.

The article, **Assumptions, Expectations, and Surprises: Teaching Autistic Children Art,** was written by Mary Adamski-Partow, who presently teaches art at Vero Beach High School in Vero Beach, Florida. Having experienced numerous professions, presently she has been in the educational field for over eight years.

Partow has presented workshops and lectures on innovative educational programs she designed and taught at national, state, and local conferences.

Dr. Rick Garner, Assistant Professor of Art Education, wrote the article, ***Art and Disabilities in the Elementary Classroom.*** Garner teaches in the School of Art and Design, at Kennesaw State University, Kennesaw, Georgia. His educational background includes degrees in studio art, psychology, art therapy, and art education. His experiences include working with technology and with individuals with disabilities. His research is in the areas of graphic development, technology in art education, and visual arts in special education.

Day Seventeen: Tuesday

LYNN'S CLASSROOM
FIFTH GRADE

AFTER SCHOOL NOTES

It is after school and I am working on my Masters Project. I am researching personality styles. It is interesting that learning styles are distinctive from personality styles. Learning styles are a distinctive way to acquire knowledge and embrace visual, audio, and kinesthetic learners. Personality styles are constructed using more broad generalizations.

According to Neil Fleming's 1987 VAK Model, Learning styles are "designed to be a starting place for a conversation among teachers and learners about learning. It can also be a catalyst for staff development - thinking about strategies for teaching different groups of learners can lead to more, and appropriate, variety of learning and teaching."

The benefit of knowing personality styles helps us understand ourselves better, and how we might react, communicate, think, or approach a situation. Carl Jung and Isabel Briggs Myers[1] developed a method of classifying types.

According to Jung's theory, "people can be characterized by their preference of general attitude:
- *Extraverted (E) vs. Introverted (I),*
- *Sensing (S) vs. Intuition (N),*
- *Thinking (T) vs. Feeling (F) and*
- *Judging (J) vs. Perceiving (P)."*

The first question is, What does that mean?

An extravert and introvert will be motivated by external or internal factors. Do you act first or reflect before acting?

Sensing and intuition deal with using facts for information, or thinking about the possibilities. Do you get all the facts first to develop a conclusion, or imagine how things could be?

In regard to thinking and feeling, which do you use, your head or your heart? Are you logical and analytical, or do you base behavior on how others are going to feel?

Finally, judging and perceiving reflect how one approaches life. Are you organized, or are you impulsive and "roll with the punches"?

After my research, I definitely wanted to know my personality type. So, I took two tests I found on the Internet at these sites: http://www.16personalities.com/personality-types and http://www.humanmetrics.com/cgi-win/jtypes2.asp. I was surprised because both tests came up with the same type, ENTP. So I am an extravert, intuitive, thinking, and perceptive individual!

My second question is, How can this information be used to enhance the effectiveness of my teaching for my students? Further reading presented itself with an idea to implement a personality styles project in the classroom—the purpose being to observe any correlation between project choice and personality style.

According to Silver and Strong (1995), when interwoven, these four types of styles provide guidelines that support curriculum development and teacher instruction. The [2]Sensory Feeler (SF) (Blue) is compassionate, people oriented, sensitive, responsive, and tolerant. The Sensory Thinker (ST) (Gold) is organized, consistent, responsible, determined, hard working, and task oriented. The Intuitive Feeler (NF) (Orange) is a risk taker, creative, innovative, active, and spontaneous. The Intuitive Thinker (NT) (Green) is analytical, logical, objective, independent, and efficient.

The following project includes two sections, the Social Studies unit on Ancient Egypt and art projects designed to correlate to Personality Styles.

PART 1

Social Studies Lesson: Social Studies Standard: NSS-WH.5 ERA 2: *Early Civilizations and the emergence of pastoral peoples, 4,000–1,000 BCE. The students will* *explore the major characteristics of civilization and how civilizations emerged in Mesopotamia, Egypt, and the Indus valley.*

Students were introduced to a YouTube video on the history of ancient Egypt, with an archaeological slant.

The title, *Egypt's Ten Greatest Discoveries,* is available at https://www.youtube.com/watch?v=uNyztf1UYJ0&index=2&list=RDKuUMe-43A3E (Retrieved December 10, 2014).

During the presentation, students were required to take notes. While viewing the presentation, periodically the video was stopped, the following questions were discussed, and the students filled in the worksheet.

Describe the land and weather of the country of Egypt.
What do archaeologists uncover?
What do archaeological "finds" tell us?
Name some famous pharaohs of Egypt.
Name some important monuments made by the Egyptians.
List some major Egyptian achievements.
Why was the Nile River important to the Egyptian people?
What was the belief system of the Egyptians?
Name some Egyptian gods and goddesses.
State the great discoveries identified in the presentation.

Personality Styles Project

Four projects related to the Egyptian culture were designed and written. The description of the art activities was printed on colored paper that corresponded to the styles. I considered this lesson as a teaching experiment.

- The Sensory Thinker / Gold project was to follow instructions for making a project.
- The Sensory Feeler / Blue project focused on activity involving feelings.
- The Intuitive Feeler / Orange project was to be inventive and use imagination.
- The Intuitive Thinker / Green project focused on research.

After the YouTube presentation, I planned to introduce the art activities related to ancient Egypt. I divided the room into four color-coordinated centers. As I moved throughout the room, I stopped at each center and explained the art activities to the students. It was announced, "You may select the project of your choice." The students moved quickly to the centers and I stayed out of their way. The students reread project descriptions and then began to work enthusiastically on their project.

ST PROJECT

The **ST project**, *How to Make Egyptian Sun-Dried Bricks*, was presented on gold paper.

Table 1 had directions and art materials to make one brick and create a display board stating the steps for making Egyptian bricks.

Directions:
1. Mix dirt and water to create a thick mud.
2. Add sand or straw and mix thoroughly.
3. In a mold, pack the mixture.
4. Set the mold out in the sun to dry (usually 2 days).

After a messy activity and the cleanup, students worked on their display board drawing and writing the procedures for making the bricks.

SF PROJECT

The **SF project**, *The Queen's Jewelry Box & Jewelry* was written on blue paper.

Table 2 students had visual resources showing a variety of Egyptian jewelry and containers.

Among the art materials (after a visit to Michaels Arts & Craft and Hobby Lobby) were containers of beads, sequins, small plastic boxes, and self-stick acrylic gems and rhinestones. Small, thin plastic shapes such as hearts, circles, and squares had holes for cording. Surfaces were glued (jewelry glue) with an assortment of the findings. Numerous jewelry kits provided materials for making earrings and bracelets.

Students made necklaces and string beaded bracelets, and decorated jewelry boxes.

Students attached their finished items with their names on to a display board and table.

NF PROJECT

The **NF project**, typed on orange paper, was to *Draw a New Species of Birds* and was based on "fossils" found during an "Egyptian Archaeological Dig."

Students used the computer to research the types of birds found in ancient Egypt. As an archaeological team, they decided to construct a new kind of bird by combining parts from three different birds of that time.

They chose the art materials to draw, design, and color a new bird species, including giving it a name.

Students (influenced by Indiana Jones) wore their hats during class and asked if they could write an adventure story as archaeologists.

NOTES

The **NT project** included research about *Egyptian Boats.* This project was presented on green paper. The computer was used to research the types of boats used in ancient Egypt.

Students drew the different boat styles and colored in with colored pencils. They found the name of a famous boat builder and wrote the name in hieroglyphics on the display board with the drawings.

They asked if they could use clay and create models of boats. Finding some air-hardening modeling clay, "Go to it" was proposed. Needless to say, they were very excited.

Students' behavior was observed. They stayed on task, worked cooperatively, and conversation pertained only to the project. Sitting back in my chair, I watched students work with enthusiasm. It was like a whirlwind. After all 28 students settled down upon completion of their projects, the results were surveyed. The number of students who selected ST project was 15, SF was 9, NF was 2, and NT was 2. Luckily, enough time was reserved for this experiment, because students were ardently involved in their projects.

The purpose for conducting this project was to be aware of the diversity of styles in the classroom, to observe students, and assess the educational value of implementing activities that incorporate Personality Styles. My research continued as I itemized a list of expectations related for each trait to be used as a future resource.

Teacher's Emphasis for Sensory Thinker

1. Expectations to be clearly stated
2. Need structure, clear procedures
3. Visual organizers, clear instructions
4. Practice skill for mastery
5. Projects to organize/sequence/categorize
6. List making and competition

Teacher's Emphasis for Sensory Feeler

1. Expectations to be clearly stated
2. Group projects/teams/pairs
3. Project concerned with sensing/feeling
4. Open ended, multi-answer activities
5. Focus on personal, social experiences

Teacher's Emphasis for Intuitive Feeler

1. Hands-on activities
2. Create new forms, 2D & 3D art projects
3. Projects—rewrite, explore alternative possibilities
4. Projects—formulate hypotheses and identify patterns

Teacher's Emphasis for Intuitive Thinker

1. Problem-solving activities in teams/pairs
2. Group projects/teams/pairs
3. Projects to compare and contrast
4. Projects for cause and effect
5. Projects to group by common characteristics
6. Projects to analyze problems—predict, interpret, and summarize information

Photographs of students while working at the centers and their display boards were recorded. Qualitative data was collected based on student interviews. Additional research material has been compiled and this teaching experiment will be the basis for my Master's Paper.

Day Eighteen: Wednesday

SHARLENE'S ART ROOM

MORNING NOTES PREPARING FOR ART WORKSHOP

Art Workshop Notes on Writing Integrating Lessons

My goal for this workshop is to introduce Visual Arts Education teaching strategies to the classroom teachers, so they can write these strategies within their lesson plans. It is important for the teachers to recognize the importance on integrating these teaching components. The following material will be handed out to faculty and discussed in today's workshop. An example of an integrated teaching unit, *Seasons*, will be sent to all teachers tomorrow.

Art Workshop in the Media Center

Sharlene's Introduction:
I wish to share with you that in the field of Art Education, the National Visual Arts Standards have been updated. So, that is why my written standards next to exhibited student artwork might have a different look. The following information speaks to the changes.

The National Art Education Association, in 2014, updated the teaching standards to reflect current issues in the field of art education. The emphasis has been on the elaboration of process embracing creating, presenting, responding, and connecting. All art standards involve the creative process of developing artistic ideas and works of art. A work of art that is generated and conceptualized is presented to be analyzed, interpreted, and appreciated, and for deeper understanding, relate and connect with societal, cultural, historical, and educational content.

Today's discussion topic is enhancing classroom lessons using Visual Arts. The following handout for discussion includes teaching strategies that you can use when writing integrated lessons. Also, now available for faculty use, an Art History resource with student artwork, located in the Art History – Art Gallery link.

HANDOUT
Writing Integrated Lessons

A teaching strategy to enhance classroom lessons is to incorporate a visual, such as an art poster, Internet slide, and display or book illustration. Visuals are an important feature as an engaging element when teaching.

Further enrich a lesson by including one or more Art Education teaching components: *Art Criticism Questions and Aesthetic Questions (responding and presenting)*, an *Art History (connecting)*, and *Art Production (creating)*.

Incorporating one of these art components when writing the lesson plan facilitates the building of additional knowledge and learning by the student. Asking stimulating Art Criticism and Aesthetic Questions when viewing visual materials intensifies activation, focus, and concentration of students. Presenting probing and penetrating questions when viewing images encourages students to perceive connections to personal experiences and memories. This action engages students' emotions and attitudes, which have a strong influence on learning and are crucial to the storage and retrieval of information (Jenson, 2000). This process of connecting new information within a personal context places students in a learning task modality, thus building knowledge and meaning as their brain translates the information into memory. Teachers use visual materials for motivating interest and discussion within lessons. This method reaches the visual learners that make up the majority of the population.

An interactive discussion between teacher and students about the image reaches the audio learners and enhances not only the acquisition of information, but also further assists students to develop verbal skills. When students confidently and eagerly walk up to the screen or an art poster, and point with their finger to answer a question, they are involved in a noteworthy experience. This activity is a memory technique that merges movement and emotion, and can reach the kinesthetic learner, along with students who like to demonstrate their knowledge and viewpoint.

The following layout is a thoughtful approach for evolving an integrated lesson. Select the discipline that you wish to teach and assess which art education component lends itself to enhance the lesson. Ask the question, *Which art component complements and merges the visual with the lesson?*

Classroom Discipline	***Art Component***
Science	Art History
Social Studies	Art Project
Math	Aesthetic Questions
Language Arts	Art Criticism Questions

ART CRITICISM QUESTIONS (RESPONDING)

The components of Feldman's Art Criticism model include Describing, Analyzing, Interpreting, and Judging works of art. The purpose of this method is to understand and appreciate works of art and clarify the role of art in society. When critiquing a work of art, employ the following questions:

1. ***Describe:*** *What things do you see in the work of art? What words would you use to describe the artwork?*

2. ***Analyze:*** *What are the dominant elements and principles of art in the work? What dominant colors or shapes did the artist use in this work of art? Does this work of art illustrate two-dimensional or three-dimensional characteristics? What is the central focus of this work?*

FIGURE 18-1

3. **Interpretation:** *What is the artist saying? What title would you give this work of art? If you could write a story about this work of art, what would you say?*
4. **Judgment:** *How do you rate the artist's technical skill? What do you like about this artwork? Do you think this artwork is worth remembering? Would you place this artwork on the wall in your home?*

AESTHETIC QUESTIONS (PRESENTING)

Aesthetics is that branch of philosophy in which questions are raised and examined about the nature, meaning, and value of art. When discussing aesthetic features of a work of art for classroom students, these questions will encourage discussion.

FIGURE 18-2

Topic: What is Art?

Must art be beautiful?
Must art be made by hand?
Must art express feelings or emotions in order to be considered art?
Can furniture be art?

FIGURE 18-3

Topic: Value of Art:

Who can say what is good art or bad art?
Can a work of art be both beautiful and ugly?
Must art be enjoyed?
Are the works of art made a long time ago more valuable?

FIGURE 18-4

NOTES

Topic: Art's Connection to Society:

If you don't like the artwork can you alter it?
Must art have a social message?
Can there be different interpretations about the same work of art?
An artifact from a past culture, is it considered art today?

FIGURE 18-5

ART HISTORY (CONNECTING)

When teaching a Social Studies unit, whether it relates to a culture or a specific historical time frame, art history provides students with an in-depth instruction by incorporating artwork of the time or culture. When studying the contextual aspect of an Art History time frame, students begin to realize the influence of social, political, religious, geographical, and philosophical ideas and events on the arts.

FIGURE 18-6

Works of art illustrate how people lived, their architecture, fashion, battles, ideas, rulers, and dreams. These images tell the story of the time or culture presenting an organic view of the life and times of people—their successes or failures. A Social Studies unit with an art history element enables students to see relationships—they are experiencing a panoramic, comprehensive presentation of information. This integrated methodology of instruction, when consistently taught, creates patterns of understanding and learning by students.

FIGURE 18-7

FIGURE 18-8

ART PRODUCTION (CREATING)

Art production is a creative activity and helps children understand other subjects much more clearly. Participation in the art making process improves academic performance, because it promotes and stimulates brain activity, creating relationships between disciplines of study. Not only does art making enhance learning, but it also supports the building blocks of a student's development. Painting or scribbling with a crayon enhances motor skills.

FIGURE 18-9

When students talk about their art, language skills are enriched with the feelings of accomplishment—they solved problems, made decisions, and took a risk in creating their art. Visual, spatial skills are developed when teachers use images or three-dimensional objects in lessons from the digital media, books, and television.

One of the most important performance-based activities for assessment in education is art production; but more important, it nurtures the development of a student's self-esteem, self-discipline, cooperation, self-motivation, and tools for communicating thoughts and ideas in a variety of ways.

According to Lisa La Saga, a video artist who created a passionate statement on *The Importance of Art Education*, *"Art enables children to be critical innovative thinkers to problem solve, express, communication, create and experiment. It is our job as a society to nurture and support the creative minds of children, in order to allow their ideas and imaginations to grow a prosperous future"* (Retrieved Jan. 3, 2015 from http://youtu.be/DAm9kEfR8GM).

FIGURE 18-10

FIGURE 18-11

ART FOR THE ELEMENTARY EDUCATOR

Day Nineteen: Thursday

SHARLENE'S ART ROOM

MORNING EMAIL
CLASSROOM TEACHERS

Email: *Faculty*
RE: *Art Workshop on Integrated Lessons*
Dear Teachers,
The following is an example of a teaching unit that integrates classroom disciplines: Math, Science, Language Arts, and Social Studies. The lessons in each discipline reference the same work of art, and integrate one of the Art Education components: Art Criticism, Aesthetics, Art Production, and Art History. The teaching unit's title is, "Four Seasons—An Integrated Teaching Unit for First Grade."

The following YouTube site is an excellent resource for introducing a lesson on seasons:
YouTube: **A Book of Seasons**
Authors: Alice and Martin Provensen @ http://youtu.be/WhDJDIviAOg
Published on Feb 20, 2013
Retrieved November 22, 2014

LESSON INTRODUCTION

Introduce students to the YouTube video about the four seasons as motivation. To further stimulate discussion about the *Four Seasons*, do a screen capture of the video's introduction picture. The teacher can screen capture the book's cover and use it to introduce the lesson.

Cover image from A Book of Seasons by Alice Provensen and Martin Provensen, published by Random House Books for Young Readers. Copyright © 1976.

(How to screen capture: if using Mac: press at the same time Command & Shift & # 4, then move mouse over image, which appears on desktop. PC computer: Press the Print Screen (⌨ PrtScr) key on your keyboard. This will capture an image of your entire screen and copy it to the clipboard.)

LESSON 1.

Math Lesson with Art Criticism Questions

As students view the picture with four seasons, ask the following art criticism questions:

- *What do you see in the picture? How many seasons do you see? How are the seasons different?*
- *What is the story in the picture? What colors, shapes, patterns, and textures did the artist use? Do you think the artist did a good job drawing and coloring the picture? Has anyone slid down a hill on a sleigh in the winter?*

Math Objective: Understand measurable attributes of objects and units, systems and the process of measurement; Use repetition of a single unit to measure something larger than the unit.

Math Project: Each student will apply the process of addition to a problem.

Math problems: The sleigh went down the hill from top to bottom in 2 minutes. The kids went down the hill 10 times. What is the total time the kids played going down the hill?

The kids picked 10 apples for one basket, and they filled 2 baskets. How many apples did they pick?

Math Assessment: Worksheet

LESSON 2.
Science Lesson with Aesthetic Questions

As students view the picture with the four seasons, ask the following aesthetic questions:
- *Looking at the four seasons, which artwork do you like best?*
- *This picture is from a YouTube video, is it art? What is your favorite part of the picture?*
- *How do you feel about your picture?*
- *What is your favorite season of the year?*
- *Do you know why we have seasons?*

Science Objective: Earth and Space Science: Weather changes from day to day and season to season. Science Project: Students will identify seasons related to the position of the Earth to the Sun and recognize seasons occur by movement around the Sun. As a resource, students are to view a model of the Earth moving around the Sun on the website.
Retrieved November 22, 2014.
http://projects.astro.illinois.edu/data/Seasons/seasons.html. (Need Flash Player)

Science Assessment: Worksheet - Write seasons

LESSON 3.
Social Studies Lesson with Historic Connection

As students view the picture with the four seasons, the teacher points out the winter scene and tells the following story: *Has anyone here been caught in a bad snowstorm called a blizzard? Well, I am going to tell you a story of a blizzard called, "The*

White Hurricane," that happened over a hundred years ago. It was a Sunday night and as the sun set, the rain turned into blinding snow. It was so cold, temperatures were below zero, the howling winds traveled one hundred miles per hour and made monstrous snowdrifts. When the snow stopped and you looked outside, you couldn't see the houses next door. Schools were closed, gas and telephone wires snapped. Many people lost their lives, and ships that were in the harbor ran aground.

*Snow removal depended on manpower and it took 17,000 workers a few days to move the snow from the streets. The snowstorm was called **The Blizzard of 1888,** and became a historical event, because it covered the entire northeastern United States.*

Retrieved November 22, 2014.
(http://themonmouthjournal.com/remembering-the-great-blizzard-of-p1714-1.htm)

Social Studies Objective: Geography
Understand how to apply geography to interpret the past: Students will identify the northeastern region in the United States.

Geography Project: Students receive a black and white handout of the United States. Students identify where they live with an "X." Following the teacher's spelling, students locate, write, and use crayons to color the five regions on the map: Northeast (Blue), Southeast (Orange), Midwest (Yellow), Southwest (Green), and West (Red).

Social Studies Assessment: Worksheet Map

LESSON 4.
Language Arts Lesson with Art Production

As students view the picture with the four seasons, the teacher asks:
What is your favorite season of the year? How is each season different? How are the trees different in each season? What activities would you do in summer, winter, fall, and spring?

Objective: Use illustrations and details in a story to describe its characters, setting, or events. Students will draw characteristics of a specific season.

Language Arts Project: Each student selects a season they like for their art project. Each drawing includes a tree (indicating seasonal characteristics) and the student engaged in a seasonal activity. Each student writes on the bottom of his or her paper, *I like (name; season) because it is (adjective).* Adjectives are written on board for students.

Language Arts Assessment: Artwork images correspond to season written on paper.

STEPS FOR DRAWING A TREE:

- Draw two curved lines for the sides of the tree.
- Draw Vs for the branches and build.
- Depending on the season, curved shapes can complete the tree and contain leaves or fruit.

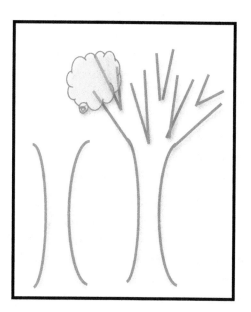

Day Twenty: Friday

SHARLENE'S ART ROOM

MORNING EMAIL
CLASSROOM TEACHERS

Email To Teachers

Hello All,

This past Wednesday was our last day for the faculty art workshops. Your attendance and participation was greatly appreciated. During the last four workshops, I have introduced four fundamental visual arts components: aesthetics, art criticism, art history, and art production. The goal for these workshops was to encourage teachers to enhance learning experiences for their students by using these educational strategies. Four lessons on Seasons were written to illustrate a realistic integration of these Visual Arts components within classroom disciplines. This material was sent to all workshop participants the following day.

Thank you for attending the workshops, and hopefully this material will be of value when writing integrated lesson.

Remember to link up to the school's Art Gallery to see the artwork in the art history section. Also, Visit the school's "ADS Art Website" where you can Ask Dear Sharlene art-related questions.

Artfully yours, Sharlene, askdearsharlene@tds.net
Art Specialist

WELCOME TO THE ADS ART WEBSITE, FINDING ANSWERS TO ART QUESTIONS

Ask Dear Sharlene

Q. Dear Sharlene,
Do you have any suggestions on classroom management techniques? Thanks, Lewanda

A. Hello Lewanda,
One of the most successful strategies for classroom management is a communication tool called the "Talking Stick." Its function is to enhance dialogue among your students, which improves listening skills and communication among your students. I've included a Talking Stick example and how to implement this project in your classroom. When participating in a circle, one student holds the Talking Stick. That student is the only one allowed to speak, while others in the circle listen. Interruptions are not permitted. Everyone in the circle who requests to speak is given the time to present their viewpoint or problem. When students have a concern and want to speak at the next meeting, they write their name on the Circle's small white board in the classroom. I suggest you hold the meeting very Friday afternoon. After students move their chairs into a circle, it is best to reviews the rules. A present-day strategy for motivating the practice of the Talking Stick in the classroom is to organize students into teams to make a talking stick as an art project (20-1). Materials include an 18-inch dowel, paint, glue, yarn, beads, and feathers. This activity will spur students' enthusiasm to participate in the Talking Stick circle. Everyone who wishes to speak is listened to. When these meetings are sustained throughout the school year, students' behavior, attitudes, values, respect, and patience are exhibited when interacting with other individuals. Hope this helps, so let me know when you do the project, and invite me.

Sharlene

FIGURE 20-1

WELCOME TO THE ADS ART WEBSITE, FINDING ANSWERS TO ART QUESTIONS

Ask Dear Sharlene

Q. Dear Sharlene,
What do you recommend for art centers in my classroom? I could use some pointers! Appreciate it! Lewanda

A. Hello Lewanda,

I find these two centers the most popular for students and teachers: the Clay Center and the Imagination Center. We know that students learn in various ways. In the Clay Center, a popular tactile activity by students is squeezing, rolling, pinching, building, and poking clay. Kept in an airtight container, the modeling clay can be reused throughout the school year. Color--coding clay with corresponding laminated color construction paper is a practical system for student use. For example, Crayola sells modeling clay in red, yellow, blue, and green colors. Assigning each group of students only one color, with laminated colored paper to use throughout the school year, will extend its usage. The reason for using this method is when students mix the colors together the clay becomes muddy looking.

An additional center is the Imagination Center where students can draw, color, design, and make puppets for the theater. Puppet shows can be held in the classroom's theater, which can be made from a large painted and decorated cardboard box with a curtain attached in the front.

This theater, as a storytelling center, is used for creative drama allowing students to work together, improve communication skills, and enrich their imagination. Pretending is so much fun! Students sharing in the art process enrich their emotional, social, cognitive, and physical development. My favorite theater art project is making a paper bag puppet. I decorate the storyteller and her wand with shiny beads, acrylic gems, and sparkles. Students love to listen to the storyteller.

Sharlene

WELCOME TO THE ADS ART WEBSITE, FINDING ANSWERS TO ART QUESTIONS

Ask Dear Sharlene

Q. Dear Sharlene,
I'm concerned about the quality of art activities I plan for my kindergarten students. How can I tell if I am teaching an art project or a craft project? Mary

A. Dear Mary,
The following is a story and some information that might help you determine your future art projects. Thanks for asking, Sharlene

"Joey was so excited as he woke up Friday morning. He was off to school, and it was Valentine's Day. It was art day! Joey could hardly keep the excitement inside as the teacher introduced the steps for making his valentine. Joey started with a red piece of construction paper and glued a paper dolie on top. Then he folded another red piece of construction paper and traced the teacher's drawing of half a heart with his pencil. He cut on his pencil line and when finished he opened it up. Bursting with pride, he had made a heart. He then followed directions and glued it on the dolie. That night Joey and his mom came to school. Excited, he dragged his mom into his classroom to show her his valentine. As they looked at the bulletin board, Joey was perplexed for he couldn't find his valentine. "I can't find my art," he cried. "They all look alike!"

This story and the following material describe characteristics of a craft center activity, focusing only on the product.
- Instructions are to be followed by the students.
- The teacher creates a sample of the project for the children to copy.
- There is only one right way to make the project.
- The children's art all looks the same.
- Patterns of examples are available online.

It is essential, as an educator, when students are involved in art activities that they can be spontaneous, creative, and express themselves using their ideas. When young students are not focused on the product, they are feeling the "process" by exploring and experimenting with art materials. "Process" is celebrated when students create a work of art that is original and uniquely theirs. As students gain confidence with art materials, they also gain confidence in creating their artwork. They begin to evaluate and rework their artwork, moving back and forth between exploring and producing.

In the lesson plan, the teacher records an art standard, sets the objectives for the art activity, introduces art language, provides materials, initiates motivation, and states assessment criteria. Art materials for an art project must be age appropriate. The teacher experiments with the materials and makes an example to evaluate suitability for student use.

It is important to give students enough time to use the materials as they focus on creating their art. A teaching environment that blends teacher-guided art activity includes actions such as presenting a theme, introducing new materials, building on existing activities, and posing a problem to students. In this environment the teacher's role is that of a facilitator. Child-initiated art activities in an early childhood art program embrace the child's eagerness to create because the art comes from within, and is reflecting personal meaning. The art might not be recognizable, but it will be unique, original, and personal. The teacher, using this approach, provides complete freedom for students' expressions and does not intervene (Schirrmacher, 2011). A teaching environment that blends teacher-guided and child-initiated instruction encourages long-term student participation in creative activities.

WELCOME TO THE ADS ART WEBSITE, FINDING ANSWERS TO ART QUESTIONS

Ask Dear Sharlene

Q. Dear Sharlene,
I want to include a landscape art project in my geography lesson. Do you have some suggestions on how to approach this project? Lynn

A. Dear Lynn,
The following material should help you with the landscape art project you'd like to do with your students. You can use oil pastels (drawing paper) or watercolor paints (watercolor paper). Let the students express themselves using color! When drawing a landscape, the student can use a horizontal or vertical format.

The image is to contain spatial characteristics: foreground, middleground, background. Lay out your design, using a pencil. Starting with the background, a suggestion, mountains; middleground can be lakes or houses, and then a foreground can show a road, ground, or flowers. Organic or geometric shapes can be used for expression. Shapes in the front are largest and overlap shapes in the middle and the background (shapes in the background are smallest).

Teacher's Art Example

Plan your colors: An **Expressionist artist uses colors based upon emotion.**

In other words, do not watercolor this art in a realistic style. For example, a tree does not have to be green and brown like you see on the right; it can be pink and purple as you see on the left. An Expressionist uses intense, bright colors.

Colors: using opposite colors on the color wheel creates intensity when placed next to each other in the art (red/green, orange/blue, yellow/purple). When completed you can if you used watercolor keep art as is, or use a sharpie and trace the shapes. If you used oil pastels, use the edge of a black oil pastel and trace all the shapes in the art.

Let me know if you need any additional information. Sharlene

WELCOME TO THE ADS ART WEBSITE, FINDING ANSWERS TO ART QUESTIONS

Ask Dear Sharlene

Q. Dear Sharlene,
In my math class, I have a lesson on patterns and would like some suggestions on an activity to make the lesson more exciting for my students.

Thanks for the help. Jerome

A. Hello Jerome,
One of my favorite art projects for making patterns is my design lesson.

I usually use a symmetrical image from science such as an insect, butterfly, or a bug. Here are the steps and art language for the project:
1. Draw with pencil, the shapes, making sure the design is a symmetrical balance; then using an X-fine Sharpie trace over pencil.
2. Draw with Sharpie, line patterns. Repeat same line three or five times, then change direction. Lines: straight,

curved, zigzag, spiral, diagonal, an original line is a combination of other lines.

3. A symmetrical design requires that the same pattern design on one side corresponds to the other (see example).

4. Shapes can be filled in with a sharpie, creating a balance with the positives and negative shapes with white and black, respectively.

5. If students fill in the shapes let them view the design from a distance, neither the black nor the white shapes are dominant, viewing it should feel balanced

6. When making the design, the more patterns, the more interesting the art. The insect, using patterns, has been <u>abstracted</u> even though we can recognize the insect by its shape.

Teacher's Art Example

ART FOR THE ELEMENTARY EDUCATOR

WELCOME TO THE ADS ART WEBSITE, FINDING ANSWERS TO ART QUESTIONS

Ask Dear Sharlene

Q. Dear Sharlene,
My students enjoy saying the rhymes you suggested. Do you have more information on how to move to some rhymes and perhaps some additional art rhymes I can use in my classroom? Mary

A. Mary,
I am pleased that your students enjoy the rhymes. Students learn best and retain information when blending mind and body. Let students enjoy choreographing movements to rhymes. Please download the following attachment and view the images for the flower rhyme, and a clock rhyme for learning time you might like.

Here are some additional art rhymes I wrote that you might like to use in your classroom when introducing an art project.

Texture
Texture here, textures there,
texture, texture, everywhere.
Rough, hard, smooth and
bumpy texture can be even
lumpy.

Primary Colors
Red, Yellow, Blue, we need
you, you're primary colors,
and you're called a hue.
All three colors make brown
ya know...
so pick up your brush, and
let's go.

Space
Space that's flat is called 2-D,
add some depth,
dimension 3.

Pattern
When we repeat, repeat,
repeat,
we make a pattern,
Pattern, pattern.

Symmetrical Balance
Symmetrical balance
is its name,
when both sides
look the same.

Note: This rhyme helps students to remember to write their name on their artwork

Put your name on the bottom
and to the right,
on the front of your art
and you'll be tight!!

ART FOR THE ELEMENTARY EDUCATOR

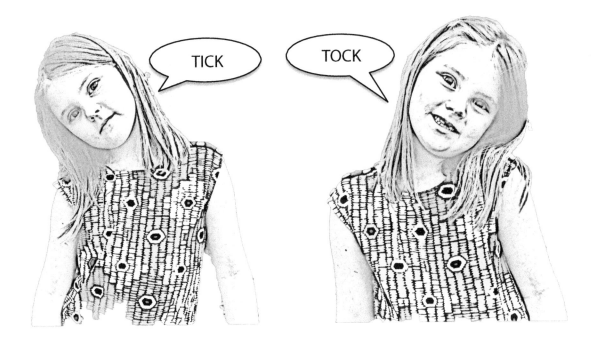

ART FOR THE ELEMENTARY EDUCATOR

WELCOME TO THE ADS ART WEBSITE, FINDING ANSWERS TO ART QUESTIONS

Ask Dear Sharlene

Q. Dear Sharlene,
I want to thank you for presenting the art workshops. My lessons are more interesting because of the art education information and lessons. Would you have any additional activities, for all teachers to reference, related to the presented materials? Esther

A. Esther,
Thanks for your positive comment. I have written a list of activities related to the content presented in the workshops and lesson plans. I will email all teachers.

Email
To: Teachers:
From: ADP website
cc: A.L., Principal
Subject: List of Activities

Hello all,
Please download the attachment that contains suggested activities related to the art education workshops. I wish to thank all the teachers for their cooperation as a team, these past weeks for the Wednesday art workshops.

Artfully Yours,
Sharlene

ACTIVITIES

All written <u>narratives</u> need to follow these requirements:
- Use WORD doc or docx
- Write one page with a minimum of 250 words
- Margins are top/bottom 1" sides 1.25"
- Use Font Cambria and size 12
- Line spacing use 1.5 and when finished
- Use *Justify Text* for final presentation.

If research is required, use APA format for resources.

Day 1 Monday:

Outer Space Adventure -Creativity in the Classroom

A. You are an immortal human being. You are able to live on any planet in this solar system. Select a planet other than Earth where you would like to live. Write a narrative about the planet you have chosen; describe the planet's environment and how you would change it to fit your personality.

B. Transformation art activity is found on page 11 in Day 1.
The activity is to transform the shape into a recognizable image, or create an imaginary item by drawing details on the shape. Fill the paper in the background and foreground, with drawings that suggest what actions are happening in the picture. Decide if color is desired, or left in a black and white format.

Day 2 Tuesday:

An Integrated Approach - Geometric Super Robot

A. Design of a *Super Geometric Robot* by drawing geometric shapes with pencil, trace with ultrafine Sharpie, and add color with crayons or colored markers. Add two superpowers by drawing those characteristics on your robot.

Day 3 Wednesday:

Art Workshop on Art Education – Importance of Art Education Connecting the Dots: Guideline for Integrating Art in Classroom Lessons

A. Write a narrative on why Art Education is an important element in the educational system; its educational impact on students; and influence on society.

Narrative

Artwork

Artwork

Narrative

B. Write an abbreviated Earth Science lesson on insects, specifically, butterflies. Include in the lesson:

1. Standards for Science and Visual Arts
2. Objectives for Science and Art Project
3. Introduction of lesson – Science content and art technique (select art technique found in Day 3)
4. Assessment for Science and Art project

Day 4 Thursday:

An Integrated Lesson - Under the Sea

A. You have a magic watch with a small silver button and when you click on it, you turn into your favorite sea creature. Write a narrative describing what sea creature you have become. What do you like about this creature? Describe your habitat. Then on 8" x 11" white drawing paper, draw and color the scene you described in your writing.

Day 5 Friday:

Role of Technology in the Classroom – Through the Lens: Photography in the Elementary School

A. Snap three photographs, using any type of technical equipment, which reflects your personality within your environment.

Day 6 Monday:

A Thematic Approach for Teaching a Cultural Unit - American Roots: Native American Culture

A. Select one of the following non-Western cultures—China, India, Inca, Japan, or Ghana in West Africa, and fill in the worksheet that contains themes and subtopics found on page 65, Day 6, on the selected culture.

Day 7 Tuesday:

An Integrated Lesson - What Time Is It? - Motivation Strategies

A. Reflect upon your life and remember a time that was filled with great happiness and write a narrative about that time. In addition, include a description of a time when you were confronted with a challenge.

Respond with a Lesson

Narrative Artwork

Artwork

Respond to the Worksheet

Narrative

Respond to
Questions

Narrative

Artwork Respond
to Questions

Artwork

Artwork

Day 8 Wednesday:

Art Workshop - Art Styles and Aesthetics
A. Select an art image from page 83 or 84, and answer the questions found on page 85.

B. Review the cultural images in Day 8 and select images and answer the questions found on page 97.

C. Survey your living environment and record by describing in detail the artwork hanging on your walls. Refer to the questions on page 85.

Day 9 Thursday:

Cultural Diversity in the Classroom - Symbols
A. Design a mandala by following directions in Day 9, then answer the definitions found on page 103.

Day 10 Friday:

Flower Garden – Collaboration
A. Draw your *Flower Garden* by outlining shapes with a pencil, then trace the shapes with extra-fine Sharpie and add color with crayons or colored pencils. Include in your garden, a minimum of six different designed flowers in different sizes growing from the grassy ground, four flying insects, and four creatures that live on the soil.

Day 11 Monday:

Looking at Lowenfeld - Art
Stages of Children's Art
A. Draw a picture of yourself, full body, using 8" x 10" white drawing paper.
   1. Search information on the Internet about body proportion: Retrieved April 11, 2015 http://design.tutsplus.com/articles/hum an--anatomy--fundamentals--basic-body-proportions--vector-18254
   2. Draw the outline of your body using a pencil.
   3. Draw clothing on the figure, your favorite outfit.
   4. Outline your shapes using an extra-fine Sharpie.
   5. Enhance your image by adding color.

Day 12 Tuesday:

Space and Time - Dinosaurs Lived a Long Time Ago *and* I'm Digging It... An Archaeological Dig
A. You have a magic watch, when you place both hands at 12:00, you are able to travel through time. Moving the large hand slows down the time. You're traveling back in time and stop time at the Mesozoic era. Before you leave on your time travel trek, you must write a list of 10 items that you need to take with you.

B. You have a pet dinosaur. Write a narrative about your dinosaur. Describe what it looks like, any special characteristics, its habits, what it eats, where it sleeps, and what verbal commands it will follow.

Day 13 Wednesday:

Art Workshop - Art Criticism: How To Talk About Art
A. Answer art criticism questions on page 137, related to the work of art (13-1) found on page 138.

B. Identify the dominant elements and principles of art in each of works of art found on pages 140-142.

C. Select your favorite work of art historical or contemporary. Review the four art criticism questions concerning that work of art and respond by writing your answers.

Day 14 Thursday:

An Integrated Lesson - Story Telling Quilts -Teaching Strategies
A. This activity has two parts, writing and illustrating a narrative. Choose any theme, fiction or nonfiction, write a story, and when completed, translate your story in a drawing onto an 8" x 8" square of white drawing paper. Draw with a pencil, outline with a sharpie, and add color or select a different art technique.

Day 15 Friday:

Classroom Learning Centers Supporting Multiple Intelligences
A. Visit this website: https://www.teacherspayteachers.com/Product/FREE-Multiple-Intelligence-Survey-for-Kids-200841. Download the free multiple intelligence survey for kids, read the directions, and take the survey to discover your strengths. Research and write a page about your multiple intelligence strengths. Keep a copy of this survey so you can help students find their own strengths.

Respond to the List

Narrative

Respond to Questions

Narrative

Narrative Artwork

Narrative

Day 16 Monday:

Special Needs – Assumptions, Expectations, and Surprises
A. "Special Needs" encompasses *Learning Disabilities (LD)*, which is a range of problems that can interfere with an individual's ability to understand, retain, or interpret what is read or heard. Select one of the following issues, then research and write an article on the subject.

Dyslexia
Dysgraphia
Dyscalculia
Auditory Processing Disorder (APD)
Perception/Visual Motor Defect
Language Processing Disorder (LPD)

Resource: http://ldaamerica.org/types-of-learning-disabilities/

Narrative

Day 17 Tuesday:

Personality Styles –What Style Are You?
A. Visit the website: http://www.16personalities.com
Answer the questionnaire and determine your personality style. Read further information on the characteristics of this style found in the website. Write a narrative using this information and confirm if the description is accurate.

Narrative

Day 18 Wednesday:

Art Workshop – Integrating Disciplines – Strategies
Respond to the following questions, A & B in a single page.
A. State the new terminology presented by the National Art Education Association for art standards.

B. Visual Arts has four Art Education teaching components used in this workbook. List and describe in detail each of those components.

Narrative

Day 19 Thursday:

Seasons - An Integrated Teaching Unit with Art Education Components
A. Draw and color four trees. Each tree portrays a different season: summer, fall, winter, and spring. (Seasonal activities can be included.)

Artwork

Art Workshops: A Summary

A. Select one of the art projects in the ADS website and create the art.

Artwork

ART FOR THE ELEMENTARY EDUCATOR

ART GALLERY

It began over 35,000 years ago, when a handprint made from red oxide and animal drawings was discovered on a cave wall in Altamira of Northern Spain. The art and artifacts of the Paleolithic era are the first images we study when we open an Art History book. The art in history is the visual account and exploration of ideas, beliefs, and activities of human endeavors. There are different methodologies on how to study Art History. The contextual approach takes into consideration the historical, artistic, religious, and societal events of the time in which the art was produced. Additional methods of study include formalism,

Cave Artists

which is the study of art based on the fundamentals of Art and Principles of Design. Iconography is the study of visual symbols and their meaning in a work of art. The artwork exhibited in the *Art Gallery - Art History* was created by Kennesaw State University education majors. Students selected an Art History period, used a contextual approach to research the period, constructed a timeline, and studied the artists of the time. Students created a work of art reflecting an artist's style, or echoed the thoughts of the time.

In the Old Stone Age
you had no fun
Searched for food
till the day was done.
Magic was used
to help our fears.
We made stone tools,
scrappers and spears.

30,000-10,000 BCE
Paleolithic-Old Stone Age

3500-539 BCE
Mesopotamia

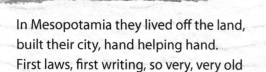 FIGURE 21-1   *Hunters*

FIGURE 21-2

Queen of Mesopotamia "My husband, Hammurabi, King of Babylon fashioned the first law codes."

In Mesopotamia they lived off the land,
built their city, hand helping hand.
First laws, first writing, so very, very old
even some art is made from gold.

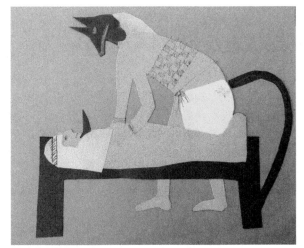

FIGURE 21-3

Anubis
"I am Anubis, God of
the dead. I am the chief
embalmer for the pharaoh."

FIGURE 21-4　　*Egyptian god*

FIGURE 21-5　　*Jeweled Collar*

The pharaoh ruled
a long time ago,
in ancient Egypt
as a god you know.
In a pyramid
their bodies did rest,
as they journey to become
Osiris in the west.

FIGURE 21-6　　*Vessel with*
Hieroglyphics

205

FIGURE 21-7 *Soldier*

Ancient Greece
unlocked many a key,
for government,
science and philosophy.
We use their ideas
even today,
their classic concepts
we still say.
Perfection in art and
temples made,
stories and myths
on them displayed.

FIGURE 21-8 *Coin*

Jeweled Collar

FIGURE 21-9

"*The Parthenon and sculptures embody the ideals of balance, harmony, order, and moderation.*"

FIGURE 21-10 *Plate with Key Design*

FIGURE 21-11   *Mosaic Design*

The Roman Empire
covered a lot,
conquered people and lands
in battles they fought.
They built roads,
 to far out places,
and there,
put their military bases.
Over 200 years
 a Caesar did rule
some were bold and
some were cruel.

FIGURE 21-12   *Mosaic Flower Design*
Mosaics are made of small cubes of different colored stone, terracotta, or glass; they decorated the floors of Roman buildings.

There is a time
called the Middle Ages,
and the history book
shows many pages.
Kings, and barons
and knights abound,
fighting the bad guy
with a frown.
People gave taxes
to harvest the land,
and in turn received,
a protecting hand.

FIGURE 21-13

Icon
"I am an icon, an image usually painted on a small wooden panel and used in devotions."

FIGURE 21-14   *Stained Glass*

FIGURE 21-15   *Religious Design*

FIGURE 21-16   *Sistine Chapel influenced Facsimile*

Renaissance is
an Italian word
that means rebirth.
A time of city-states and
classic ideas to unearth.
New ideas, with man
at the center,
The study of science,
and da Vinci as inventor.
Music, art and literature
exploded on the scene,
People really advanced
in century fifteen.

FIGURE 21-17   *Sun and Moon*
The creation of the sun and the moon is found in Michelangelo's Sistine Chapel ceiling, depicting the third and fourth day of the Creation narrative.

FIGURE 21-18   *Flower with Butterflies*

FIGURE 21-19   *Line and Emotion*

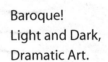

Baroque!
Light and Dark,
Dramatic Art.

FIGURE 21-20

Flowers in Motion

During this Age of Enlightenment, events included the Industrial Revolution, philosophical and scientific triumphs, and numerous inventions.

ART FOR THE ELEMENTARY EDUCATOR

FIGURE 21-21   *Sea Storm*

Romantic art, a time of emotion,
proud of the land with much devotion.
Romantic art, a time of emotion,
using imagination with much motion.

FIGURE 21-22   *Mermaid*
"I am legendary. I am the subject of fairy tales and myths, told in many cultures world-
wide and throughout history."

FIGURE 21-23   *Landscape*

FIGURE 21-24   *Grrrr*

"Realism was a reaction to Romanticism. It was a movement to depict realistic commonplace scenes of the working class, café scenes, and included realistic portraits."

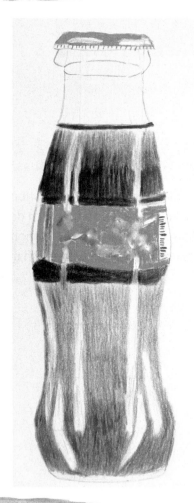

FIGURE 21-25   *Refreshing*

FIGURE 21-26   *Main Street*

Realistic art looks really real,
using values makes the deal.
Space looks 3-D, with great appeal,
that's why some art, looks really, real.

Reflecting light
during the day
gave the artists
a new way to play
by viewing the world
in a new way.
Yes, Impressionists
were here to stay.

FIGURE 21-27   *Lily Pad*

FIGURE 21-28   *Sunset*

FIGURE 21-29

Tweet, Tweet "I was painted by an Impressionist, who used short, quick brushstrokes, capturing how the light enriched the color of my feathers. Impressionists painted outdoors to capture moments in everyday life activities."

Each artist
had a different look
painting styles
for the Art History book.

Van Gogh applied
thick whirling paint:
Gauguin in Tahiti
liked nature quaint.

Cézanne created
original landscapes
by painting basic
geometric shapes.

Seurat's art
contained a thousand dots
Post Impressionists',
changed art a lot.

FIGURE 21-30   *Van Gogh's Influence*

FIGURE 21-31   *Flowers*

FIGURE 21-32   *Landscape*

The natural world shown as a cone,
Picasso began an art style unknown.
Abstracting shapes within a frame,
Cubism is the style, that's its name.

FIGURE 21–33   *Together*

FIGURE 21–34   *Viewpoint*

*"My body has been broken up into different
angles and shapes. This approach is the first
stage of the Cubist movement, called Analytical Cubism. The second stage, Synthetic
Cubism, introduced the addition of materials
for making a collage."*

FIGURE 21–35   *Cubed*

It's all in your head they said, they said,
as the artist painted dreams in his head.
A landscape painted with a melting
    clock,
and a couple floating gracefully with
    livestock.
Superior reality was the movement's
    strategy,
of Surrealism with artists like, Chagall
    and Dali.

An Icon
"I am the famous melting clock featured in Dali's painting, The Persistence of Memory (1931). I symbolize the passing of time experience while dreaming."

FIGURE 21-36

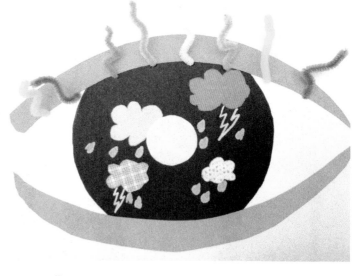

FIGURE 21-38 *I See*

FIGURE 21-37 *Everything*

A canvas made from dripping paint,
showing feelings and emotions unrestraint.
Not painted by accident, or by chance,
this canvas was planned, during the art dance.

Abridged

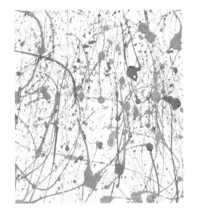

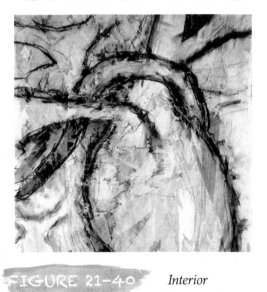

FIGURE 21-40 *Interior*

FIGURE 21-41

Drip 1

FIGURE 21-42

Drip 2

FIGURE 21-43

Movement

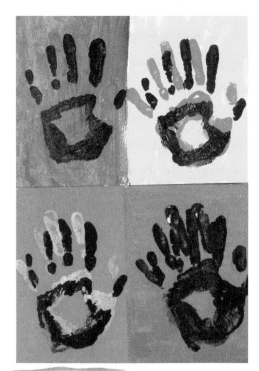

FIGURE 21-44   *Hand - Squared*

FIGURE 21-45   *Thirsty Anyone?*

They said art is everywhere
so goes the pop artists' call.
Warhol soup cans and movie stars,
hanging on the galleries wall.

FIGURE 21-46   *Music to the Beat*

FIGURE 21-47   *Rover*

Pop art was a response to the institution of fine arts. Pop art was based on popular, commonplace objects and people in everyday life.

ART FOR THE ELEMENTARY EDUCATOR

Woman's art is never done,
cause we're stitch'n and paint'n
from sun to sun.

Our art tells a story
about great artists in
all their glory.

In museums you can see
walls filled with talent
for woman's art history.

FIGURE 21-48   *Women Can be Beautiful*

FIGURE 21-49   *Tough Yet Sexy*

FIGURE 21-50   *I Can Choose*

FIGURE 21-51   *Variation of a Sports Event*

FREE ♡ AND

SOCIAL ACCEPTANCE!

PEER ENVY SOLD SEPRATELY

FIGURE 21-52

Viewpoint

FIGURE 21-53   *Oops*

Postmodern Art is hard
    to explain,
so many opinions you
    could go insane.
Deconstruct, reconstruct
    and appropriate,
value each theory so you
    can appreciate.

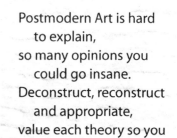

FIGURE 21-54   *Designer Fish*

ART FOR THE ELEMENTARY EDUCATOR

REFERENCES

National Visual Arts Standards. (2014). Retrieved May 9, 2015 from http://nationalartsstandards.org
(This resource was used for all art standards in this workbook.)

INTRODUCTION

Jensen, E. (2001). *Arts with the Brain in Mind.* Alexandria, VA: Association for Supervision and Curriculum Development.

DAY 1

Tate, M. (2008). *Keynote Address at TAG.T.* Retrieved September 25, 2014 from http://coppellgifted.org/2008/12/16/marcia-tate-keynote-address-at-tagt/

Tate, M. (2003). *Worksheets Don't Grow Dendrites: 20 Instructional Strategies That Engage the Brain.* Retrieved September 25 2014 from http://www.literacy-lane.org/pdfs/Tate-Strategies.pdf

The Daily Galaxy. (2012). Retrieved September 25, 2014 from http://www.dailygalaxy.com/my_weblog/2012/06/two-new-alien-planets-discovered-in-andromeda-resets-the-bar-for-weird.html

The KidsKnowIt Network. (2014). Retrieved Sept 25, 2014 from http://www.kidsastronomy.com/index.htm

Beghetto, R., & Kaufman, J. (2013). Fundamentals of Creativity. *Educational Leadership, 70*(5), 10-15.

Eckhoff, A., & Urbach, J. (2008). Understanding imaginative thinking during childhood: Sociocultural conceptions of creativity and imaginative thought. *Early Childhood, 36,* 179-185.

Hennessey, B., & Amabile, T. (2010). Creativity. *Annual Review of Psychology, 61,* 569-598.

Henriksen, D., Keenan, S., Richardson, C., & Mishra, P. (2015). Rethinking technology & creativity in the 21st century: Modeling as a trans-disciplinary formative skill and practice. *TechTrends: Linking Research & Practice to Improve Learning, 59*(3), 5-10.

Kaufman, J., & Beghetto, R. (2009). Beyond big and little: The four C model of creativity. *Review of General Psychology, 13,* 1-12.

Mishra, P., Koehler, M., & Henriksen, D. (2011). The seven trans-disciplinary habits of mind: Extending the TPACK framework towards 21st century learning. *Educational Technology, 51*(2), 22-28.

Root-Bernstein, R.S., & Root-Bernstein, M.M. (1999). *Sparks of Genius: The Thirteen Thinking Tools of the World's Most Creative People.* New York: Palgrave Macmillan.

Runco, M. (2003). Education for creative potential. *Scandinavian Journal of Educational Research, 47*(3), 317-324.

Runco, M. (2008). Creativity and education. *New Horizons in Education, 56*(1), 8.

Runco, M., & Richards, R. (1998). *Eminent Creativity, Everyday Creativity, and Health.* Norwood, NJ: Ablex.

DAY 2

Jacobs, H.H. (2004). *Workshop: Interdisciplinary Learning in Your Classroom: Concept to Classroom.* Retrieved September 26, 2014 from http://www.thirteen.org/edonline/concept2class/ interdisciplinary/index.html

ART FOR THE ELEMENTARY EDUCATOR

NOTES

NOTES

DAY 3

Catterall, J.S., Dumais, S., & Hampden-Thompson, G. (2012). The arts and achievement in at-risk youth: Findings from four longitudinal studies. *National Endowment for the Arts Report*, vol. 55.

Flanagan, A. (2009). Why students need arts education. *Arts for LA*. Retrieved November 20, 2014 from http://www.artsforla.org/why-students-need-arts-education

Florida, R. (2005). *The Flight of the Creative Class: The New Global Competition for Talent.* New York: Harper Business.

Maeda, John (2013). STEM + Art = STEAM. *The STEAM Journal, 1*(1), article 34. DOI: 10.5642/steam.201301.34. Retrieved December 3, 2014 from http://scholarship.claremont.edu/steam/vol1/iss1/34.

Pink, D.H. (2006). *A Whole New Mind: Why Right-Brainers Will Rule the Future.* New York: Riverhead Books.

Root-Bernstein, R., & Root-Bernstein, M. (1999). *Sparks of Genius. The Thirteen Thinking Tools of the World's Most Creative People.* New York: Houghton Mifflin Co.

UNESCO. (2013). *United Nations Creative Economy Report, Special Report 2013.* Retrieved February, 23, 2013 from http.://www.unesco.org/new/en/culture/themes/creativity/creative-economy-report-2013-special-edition/

DAY 4

Wachtman, J. (1995). Figures 4-1, 4-2, 4-3 Original photographs. Chattanooga, TN: Tennessee Aquarium.

Teaching Great Lakes Science. (n.d.). Retrieved October 1, 2014 from http://www.miseagrant.umich.edu/lessons/lessons/by-broad-concept/life-science/fish-life-cycle/

DAY 5

aesthetics. (n.d.). *Dictionary.com Unabridged.* Retrieved June 17, 2015 from Dictionary.com website: http://dictionary.reference.com/browse/aesthetics

Avedon. R. (n.d.). *About.* Retrieved February 22, 2015 from http://www.avedonfoundation.org/about/

Civil War Trust. (2014). Retrieved February 22, 2015 from http://www.civilwar.org/education/history/biographies/ matthew-brady.html

Perry, D. (n.d.). *Teaching with Documents: The Civil War as Photographed by Matthew Brady.* Retrieved February 22, 2015 from http://www.archives.gov/education/lessons/brady-photos/

DAY 6

Caine, R.N., & Caine, G. (1994). *Making Connections: Teaching and the Human Brain.* Menlo Park, CA: Addison-Wesley.

Caine, R.N., Caine, G., & Crowell, S. (1994). *Mindshifts: A Brain-Based Process for Restructuring School and Renewing Education.* Tucson, AZ: Zephyr Press.

Great Plains Indians. (n.d.). Retrieved October 9, 2014 from http://www.warpaths2peacepipes.com/native-american-indians/great-plains-indians.htm

Gutenberg's Myths and Legends of the Great Plains. Retrieved October 12, 2014 from http://www.gutenberg.org/files/22083/22083-h/22083-h.htm

Harnew, S. (1997). A *Teachers Workshop.* Atlanta, GA: The High Museum of Art.

Kovalik, S. (1989). *ITI Integrated Thematic Instruction.* Oak Creek, AZ: Susan Kovalik & Associates.

Kovalik, S., & Olsen, K. (1994). *ITI: The Model, Integrated Thematic Instruction.* Kent, WA: Kovalik & Associates.

National Council for the Social Studies (NCSS), Curriculum Standards for Social Studies. Retrieved October 8, 2014 from http://www.mhschool.com/socialstudies/2009/teacher/pdf/ncss.pdf

Wachtman, J. (1996). *The How of It: A Cultural Program Resource Guide.* Ball Ground, GA: RaJean and Company.

Wachtman, J. (2009). Figure 6-1 Original photograph. Machu Picchu, Peru.

Wachtman, J. (2009). Figure 6-3 Original photograph. Cusco, Peru: The Center for Traditional Textiles.

Wachtman, J. (2009). Figures 6-2, 6-4, 6-7, 6-8, 6-9 Original photographs. Lima, Peru: Larco Museum.

Wachtman, J. (2009). Figure 6-5 Original photograph. Island of Taquile, located on the Peruvian side of Lake Titicaca.

Wachtman, J. (2009). Figure 6-10 Original photograph. Puno, Peru: Coca Museum.

DAY 7

Hamilton, M., & Weiss, M. (2005). *The Power of Storytelling in the Classroom.* Retrieved March 3, 2015 from https://www.rcowen.com/PDFs/CTS%20Ch%201%20for%20website.pdf

Herberholz, D.B. (1998). *ART WORKS for Elementary Teachers.* New York: McGraw-Hill.

Koster, J.B. (2014). *Growing Artists* (6th ed.). Stamford, CT: Cengage Learning.

Mayesky, M. (2015). *Creative Activities and Curriculum for Young Children.* Stamford, CT: Cengage Learning.

Schirrmacher, R., & Fox, J.E. (2011). *Art and Creative Development for Young Children* (7th ed.). Stamford, CT: Wadsworth Cengage Learning.

Tate, M.L. (2003). *Worksheets Don't Grow Dendrites: 20 Instructional Strategies That Engage the Brain.* Thousand Oaks, CA: Corwin Press.

DAY 9

Chalmers, F.G. (1997). *Celebrating Pluralism: Art, Education, and Cultural Diversity.* Los Angeles: The Getty Institute for the Arts.
This book is currently out of print; however, it can still be easily found through book buying searches on the Internet.

Education World. (2015). Retrieved March. 1, 2015 from http://www.educationworld.com/standards/national/soc_sci/ world_history/5_12.shtml#sthash.uMkrPuPy.dpuf

Education World. (2015). Retrieved March 1, 2015 from http://www.educationworld.com/standards/national/toc/#sthash.sqN14IOX. dpuf

Geometric Symbolism. Boundless Art History. Boundless, 20 Jan. 2015. Retrieved March 1, 2015 from https://www.boundless.com/arthistory/textbooks/boundless-art-history-textbook/deities-and-places-of-worship-13/places-of-worship-92/geometric-symbolism-452-10766/

DAY 10

Common Ground: Teaching Kids the Benefits of Working Together. (2014). Retrieved March 19, 2015 from http://www.edutopia.org/common-ground

Erlauer, L. (2015). *The Brain Compatible Classroom: Using What We Know About Learning to Improve Teaching.* Retrieved February 1, 2015 from http://www.commoncoreprinciples.com/brain-compatible-classroom/

Kindergarten Science. (2014). Retrieved January 31, 2014 from http://colaborativelearning.pbworks.com/w/page/32112575/ Kindergarten%20 Science

Kovalik, S., & Olsen, K. (1993). *ITI: The Model, Integrated Thematic Instruction* (2nd ed.). Federal Way, WA: Susan Kovalik & Associates.

Nine Brain-Compatible Elements That Influence Learning. (1995). Retrieved February 1, 2015 from http://www.hope.edu/academic/education/wessman/unit5/braincompatible.htm

DAY 11

Broom, K. *Psychology Theory, Children Art.* Retrieved September 17, 2014 from http://www.users.totalise.co.uk/~kbroom/Lectures/children.htm

Englebright Fox, J., & Schirrmacher, R. (2012). *Art and Creative Development for Young Children* (7th ed.). University of Houston–Victoria.

Lowenfeld, V. (1947). *Lowenfeld's Stages of Artistic Development.* Retrieved September 17, 2014 from http://www.arteducationstudio.com/viktor.htm

DAY 12

Education World. (2015). Retrieved March 5, 2015 from http://www.educationworld.com/standards/national/soc_sci/world_history/5_12.shtml

List of Dinosaur Genera. (2015). Retrieved March 9, 2015 from http://en.wikipedia.org/wiki/List

Time for Learning. (2015). Retrieved March 14, 2015 from http://www.time4learning.com/education/third_grade.shtml #third_ss

Zoom the Dinosaurs. (2015). Retrieved March 14, 2015 from http://www.enchantedlearning.com/subjects/dinosaurs/

Video Resources:

Denizens of the Mesozoic. (2007). MissingPieces4U. Retrieved March 8, 2015 from http://youtu.be/8g5eJ0cmF84
History of the Mesozoic and its favorite inhabitants, the dinosaurs! Animated with many images of dinosaurs. 10:06 minutes best viewed on small screen

Mesozoic Era, The Time of the King. (2012). MARTINEZZZ365. Retrieved March 8, 2015 from http://youtu.be/D3MI7BkFdUI
An overview video that describes the three periods and dinosaurs in Mesozoic era. 5 minutes

Passantino, F. *What Is a Fossil?* (2011). Retrieved March 8, 2015 from http://youtu.be/3rkGu0BItKM
Fossils are the stone remains of animals or plants that were once alive. Fossils can be the bones of a dead dinosaur or his big footprints in the sand. Usually only the skeletons of animals are left after millions of years. But sometimes a whole animal, like a woolly mammoth, gets trapped in ice. 2:34 minutes

DAY 13

Bates, J.K. (2000). *Becoming an Art Teacher.* Belmont, CA: Wadsworth/Thompson Learning.

Day, M., & Hurwitz, A. (2007). *Children and Their Art: Methods for the Elementary School.* Belmont, CA: Thomson Higher Education.

Diepeveen, L., & Laar, T.V. (2001). *Art with a Difference: Looking at Difficult and Unfamiliar Art.* New York: McGraw-Hill Higher Education.

Expressionism. The Art Story.Org. (2013). Retrieved February 1, 2015 from http://www.theartstory.org/definition-formalism.htm

Kaires, J. (2012). *Aesthetic Theories*. Retrieved January 31, 2015 from http://web.fscj.edu/Joy.Kairies/tutorials_2012/art_tutorial_1/index.html

Lankford, E.L. (1992). *Aesthetics: Issues and Inquiry*. Reston, VA: National Art Education Association.

Larmer, B. (2012). Terra-cotta army: True colors. *National Geographic*. Retrieved February 2, 2015 from http://ngm.nationalgeographic.com/2012/06/terra-cotta-warriors/larmer-text

Roach, J. (n.d.). Terra-cotta army protects first emperor's tomb. *National Geographic*. Retrieved February 2, 2015 from http://science.nationalgeographic.com/science/archaeology/ emperor-qin/

Simpson, J.K., Delaney, J.M., Carroll, K.L., Hamilton, C.M., Kay, S.I., Kerlavage, M.S., & Iksibm, H.L. (1998). *Creating Meaning Through Art: Teacher as Choice Maker*. Columbus, OH: Merrill Prentice Hall.

Stewart, M. (1997). *Thinking Through Aesthetics*. Worchester, MA: Davis Publications, Inc.

Wolf, J. (2015). *The Art Story.Org - Formalism in Modern Art*. Retrieved February 1, 2015 from http://www.theartstory.org/definition-formalism.htm

Vial, D. (2014). *Ways of seeing: Imitationalism*. Retrieved January 31, 2015 from https://sites.google.com/site/yr10visualarts/ways-of- seeing-imationalism

DAY 14

Common Core: ELA Literacy. (2015). Retrieved April 1, 2015 from http://www.corestandards.org/ELA-Literacy/L/2/

Doyle, D. (2008). *Artist Profile: Faith Ringgold*. Retrieved April 1, 2015 from http://www.ndoylefineart.com/ringgold.html

EDSITEment! *Stories in Quilts*. (2010). Retrieved April 1, 2015 from http://edsitement.neh.gov/lesson-plan/stories-quilts

Gardner, H. (1983). *Frames of Mind: The Theory of Multiple Intelligences*. New York: Basic Books.

Jensen, E. (2008). *Brain-Based Learning: The New Paradigm of Teaching*. Thousand Oaks, CA: Corwin Press.

Story Quilts – A PowerPoint Presentation Illustrating the History of Quilt Making. (2010). Retrieved April 1, 2015 from http://helenrindsberg.myiglou.com/StudioCourse/FAQ00015.htm

Tate. M. (2003a). *20 Instructional Strategies That Really Work!*
Retrieved April 1, 2015 from http://www.literacylane.org/pdfs/Tate-Strategies.pdf

Tate, M.L. (2003b). *Worksheets Don't Grow Dendrites: 20 Instructional Strategies That Engage the Brain.* Thousand Oaks, CA: Corwin Press.

Willis, J. (2011). *The Brain-Based Benefits of Writing for Math and Science Learning.* Retrieved April 1, 2015 from http://www.edutopia.org

DAY 15

Chandler, L. (2011). *Multiple Intelligence Survey for Kids.* Retrieved February 4, 2015 from https://www.teacherspayteachers.com/Product/FREE- Multiple-Intelligence-Survey-for-Kids-200841

Concept to Classroom. (2004). Retrieved January 22, 2015 from http://www.thirteen.org/edonline/concept2class/mi/index_sub7.hml

Genius. (2015). Retrieved January 22, 2015 from http://www.cse.emory.edu/sciencenet/mismeasure/genius/ research02.html

Learning Styles. (2014). Retrieved November 20, 2014 from http://www.ldpride.net/learningstyles.mi.htm

Multiple Intelligences, Genius. Retrieved January 22, 2015 from http://www.tecweb.org/styles/gardner.html

Multiple Intelligences, Instructional Techniques and Activities. (2014). Retrieved January 25, 2015 from http://www.saisd.net/admin/curric/sstudies/handson/multintell.pdf

Strauss, V. (2013). *Howard Gardner: 'Multiple intelligences' Are Not 'Learning Styles.'* Retrieved November 20, 2014 from http://www.washingtonpost.com/blogs/answer-sheet/wp/2013/10/16/howard-gardner-multiple-intelligences-are-not-learning-styles/

DAY 16

Grand, T. (2012). *TAKEPART.* Retrieved February 16, 2015 from http://www.takepart.com/article/2012/08/15/temple-grandin-reveals-advice-educating-autistic-kids

DAY 17

Bible History Daily, How to Make a Mudbrick. (2014). Retrieved Dec 10, 2014 from http://www.biblicalarchaeology.org/daily/ancient-cultures/daily-life-and-practice/how-to-make-a-mudbrick/

Education World, Era 2. (2014). Retrieved December 10, 2014 from http://www.educationworld.com/standards/national/soc_sci/world_history/5_12.shtml#sthash.FuvvOn67.dpuf

Neil Fleming VAK Model Learning Styles. (2011). Retrieved December 10, 2014 from http://wiki.ggc.edu/wiki/Neil_Fleming

Personality Types Explained. (2007-2014). Retrieved December 10, 2014 from http://www.humanmetrics.com/hr/you/personalitytype.aspx

16 Personalities. (2014). Retrieved December 10, 2014 from http://www.16personalities.com/personality-types

The Myers & Briggs Foundation. (2014). Retrieved December 10, 2014 from http://www.myersbriggs.org

[1]Isabel Briggs Myers, a researcher and practitioner of Jung's theory, proposed to see the judging-perceiving relationship as a fourth dichotomy influencing personality type [Briggs Myers, 1980]

[2] *The Thoughtful Education Model.* (1995). Notes from workshop presented by Silver, Strong & Associates in Atlanta, Georgia.

DAY 18

Arnheim, R. (1989). *Thoughts on Art Education.* Los Angeles: The Getty Center for Education in the Arts.

Feldman, E.B. (1987). *Varieties of Visual Experience.* New York: H. N. Abrams Inc.

Jensen, E. (2000). *Brain-Based Learning.* San Diego: The Brain Store.

Lynch, G. (2015). *The Importance of Art in Child Development.* Retrieved January 3, 2015 from http://www.pbs.org/parents/education/music-arts/the-importance-of-art-in-child-development/

Newton, C. (2015). *Aesthetic Questions.* Retrieved January 3, 2015 from https://ntieva.unt.edu

Mulder-Slater, A. (2014). *Why Is Art Education Important?* Retrieved January 3, 2015 from http://www.kinderart.com/artspeak/important.shtml

National Visual Arts Standards. (2015). Retrieved January 3, 2015 from http://www.arteducators.org/store/NAEA_Natl_Visual_ Standards1.pdf

Saga, L. La. (2009). *The Importance of Art Education.* Retrieved January 3, 2015 from http://youtu.be/DAm9kEfR8GM

Visual Learning Style. (2012). Retrieved January 1, 2015 from http://metisl.com/visual-learning-style/

DAY 19

Education World. (2014) Retrieved November 22, 2014 from http://www.educationworld.com/standards/national/soc_sci/geography/k_12.shtml#nss-g.k-12.2

How Stuff Works. 2014. Retrieved November 22, 2014 from http://science.howstuffworks.com/nature/climate-weather/storms/10-biggest-snowstorms1.htm

Provensen, A., & Provensen, M. *A Book of Seasons.* (2013). Retrieved November 22, 2014 from http://youtu.be/WhDJDIviAOg

DAY 20

Have an art question? Email your question to:askdearsharlene@tds.net
An art specialist will answer your question.

Littleton, J. (2011). *The Caine and Caine Brain; 12 Principles of Learning.* Retrieved May 2, 2015 from http://www.examiner.com/article/the-caine-and-caine-brain-12-principles-of-learning

Page, K. (n.d.). *Teacher Directed Activities*. Retrieved May 2, 2015 from http://www.ehow.com/list_6543848_teacher-directed-activities.html

Schirrmacher, R., & Fox, J.E. (2011). *Art and Creative Development for Young Children* (7th ed.). Stamford, CT: Wadsworth Cengage Learning.

Talking Sticks. (2015). Retrieved May 2, 2015 from http://www.warpaths2peacepipes.com/native-american-culture/talking-sticks.htm

Art History Resources

Ancient Egypt. (2014). Retrieved November 4, 2014 from
http://en.wikipedia.org/wiki/Art_of_ancient_Egypt

Contributions of Mesopotamia. (2014). Retrieved November 3, 2014 from
http://www.dl.ket.org/humanities/connections/class/ancient/mesop.htm

Esaak, S. (2014). *What Is Paleolithic Art?* Retrieved November 3, 2014 from
http://arthistory.about.com/cs/arthistory10one/a/paleolithic.htm

Greek Art. (2014). Retrieved November 4, 2014 from http://en.wikipedia.org/wiki/Greek_art

Medieval Religion. (2014) Retrieved November 5, 2014 from
http://www.medieval-life-and-times.info/medieval-religion/

The Renaissance. (2014). Retrieved November 7, 2014 from
http://en.wikipedia.org/wiki/The_Renaissance

Why We Study the History of Art? Retrieved May 8, 2015 from
http://www.docstoc.com/docs/171219508/vinf-o-whyAH

The Art Story.org - Your Guide to Modern Art. (2013). Retrieved May 2 through 28, 2015 from http://www.theartstory.org/section_movements.htm
This resource provides a quick view and a detail view of information for numerous art movements.

PHOTO CREDITS

BRIDGE PHOTO (Dedication): Courtesy of Jeanette Wachtman

Day 1

FIGURE 1-1: Contributed by Fernando Rosellon. Copyright © Kendall Hunt Publishing Company.

FIGURE 1-2: Contributed by Alondra Mercoda. Copyright © Kendall Hunt Publishing Company.

FIGURE 1-3: Contributed by Briana Orellana. Copyright © Kendall Hunt Publishing Company.

Day 2

PRE-BELL-MAN STATUE: Photo: © Dieter Herwig / MSPT / Museum f,r Kommunikation. Art in photo: © Nam June Paik estate. Used with permission.

FIGURE 2-2: Contributed by Coryell Dorrough. Copyright © Kendall Hunt Publishing Company.

FIGURE 2-3: Contributed by Rokiyah Darbo. Copyright © Kendall Hunt Publishing Company.

FIGURE 2-4: Contributed by Stephanie Berry. Copyright © Kendall Hunt Publishing Company.

Day 3

AUTHOR BUTTERFLY DRAWINGS; FIGURES 3-1 TO 3-22: Courtesy of Jeanette Wachtman

Day 4

FIGURE 4.1 JELLYFISH; FIGURE 4.2 SEAHORSE; FIGURE 4.3 CORAL: Courtesy of the Tennessee Aquarium Museum.

FIGURE 4-4: Contributed by Juliana Barret. Copyright © Kendall Hunt Publishing Company.

FIGURE 4-5: Contributed by Sandi Glidewell. Copyright © Kendall Hunt Publishing Company.

FIGURE 4-6: Contributed by Maia Alison. Copyright © Kendall Hunt Publishing Company.

UNDER THE SEA DRAWINGS: Courtesy of Jeanette Wachtman

Day 5

TREE PHOTO (FIGURE 5-1) & SWING PHOTO (FIGURE 5-3): Contributed by Rebecca Tucker. Copyright © Kendall Hunt Publishing Company.

CHAIN PHOTO [FIGURE 5-2]: Contributed by Hally D'Alessio. Copyright © Kendall Hunt Publishing Company.

Day 6

ILLUSTRATION BY HUACA PUCLLANA MUSEUM: JosÈ Salazar, 2005. Museo de Sitio Huaca Pucllana.

FIGURES 6-1, 6-2, 6-5, 6-6, 6-14: Courtesy of Jeanette Wachtman

FIGURE 6-3 and FIGURE 6-4: Museo Larco. Lima—Perú

FIGURE 6-10: Courtesy of Jeanette Wachtman

FIGURE 6-11: Contributed by Emily Feste. Copyright © Kendall Hunt Publishing Company.

FIGURE 6-12: Contributed by Emelia Dettner. Copyright © Kendall Hunt Publishing Company.

FIGURE 6-13: Contributed by Hannah Gresham. Copyright © Kendall Hunt Publishing Company.

FIGURE 6-15: Contributed by Colton Pence. Copyright © Kendall Hunt Publishing Company.

Day 7

FIGURE 7-1: Contributed by Estefani Marariegos. Copyright © Kendall Hunt Publishing Company.

FIGURE 7-2: Contributed by Yocelin Garcia. Copyright © Kendall Hunt Publishing Company.

FIGURE 7-3: Contributed by Harim Sanchez. Copyright © Kendall Hunt Publishing Company.

Day 8

FIGURE 8-1: Contributed by Carmen Zayas. Copyright © Kendall Hunt Publishing Company.

FIGURE 8-2: Contributed by Aalijah Herwkins. Copyright © Kendall Hunt Publishing Company.

FIGURE 8-3: Contributed by Amya Kemp. Copyright © Kendall Hunt Publishing Company.

FIGURE 8-4: Contributed by Rachel Slater. Copyright © Kendall Hunt Publishing Company.

FIGURE 8-5: Contributed by Dakotah Sweeney. Copyright © Kendall Hunt Publishing Company.

FIGURES 8-6, 8-7, 8-20, 8-21; Contributed by Mary Adamski-Parton. Copyright © Kendall Hunt Publishing Company.

FIGURES 8-8, 8-9, 8-10 TO 8-19: Courtesy of Jeanette Wachtman
FIGURES 8-22 AND 8-23: Contributed by Sandra P. Thomas. Copyright © Kendall Hunt Publishing Company.

Day 9

FIGURE 9-1: Contributed by Lauren Bell. Copyright © Kendall Hunt Publishing Company
FIGURE 9-2: Contributed by Kevin Pham. Copyright © Kendall Hunt Publishing Company.
FIGURE 9-3: Contributed by Zayna Akan. Copyright © Kendall Hunt Publishing Company.

Day 10

FIGURE 10-1: Contributed by Dhara Patel. Copyright © Kendall Hunt Publishing Company.
FIGURE 10-1 FLOWER GARDEN: Contributed by Olivia Hancock. Copyright © Kendall Hunt Publishing Company.
FIGURE 10-1 FLOWER GARDEN: Contributed by Lynssey Johnson. Copyright © Kendall Hunt Publishing Company.
FIGURE 10-2: Contributed by Kathleen Zupo. Copyright © Kendall Hunt Publishing Company.
FIGURE 10-2: Contributed by Hannah Lee. Copyright © Kendall Hunt Publishing Company.
FIGURE 10-2: Contributed by Mark Fancellas. Copyright © Kendall Hunt Publishing Company.
FIGURE 10-2: Contributed by Jack Douglas Landrum. Copyright © Kendall Hunt Publishing Company.
FIGURE 10-3: Contributed by Tea Ziagliara. Copyright © Kendall Hunt Publishing Company.
FIGURE 10-3: Contributed by Michael Wise. Copyright © Kendall Hunt Publishing Company.
FIGURE 10-3: Contributed by Aril Kudumula. Copyright © Kendall Hunt Publishing Company.

Day 11

FIGURE 11-1: Contributed by Kim Thi Nguyen. Copyright © Kendall Hunt Publishing Company.
FIGURE 11-2: Contributed by Sandy Blackwell. Copyright © Kendall Hunt Publishing Company.
FIGURE 11-3: Contributed by Samuel Londono. Copyright © Kendall Hunt Publishing Company.
FIGURES 11-4 AND 11-10: Contributed by Ava Wachtman. Copyright © Kendall Hunt Publishing Company.
FIGURE 11-5: Contributed by Jorge Rendon. Copyright © Kendall Hunt Publishing Company.
FIGURE 11-6: Contributed by Eva Gaona. Copyright © Kendall Hunt Publishing Company.
FIGURES 11-7 AND 11-8: Contributed by Hayden Wachtman. Copyright © Kendall Hunt Publishing Company.
FIGURE 11-9: Contributed by Leilani Krajewski. Copyright © Kendall Hunt Publishing Company.
FIGURE 11-11: Contributed by Haylee Donley. Copyright © Kendall Hunt Publishing Company.
FIGURE 11-12: Contributed by Mason Breeze. Copyright © Kendall Hunt Publishing Company.

Day 12

FIGURE 12-1 BIG DINO: Contributed by Fransisco Talamantes Caldera. Copyright © Kendall Hunt Publishing Company.
FIGURES 12-2, 12-3, 12-4, 12-5, AND 12-6: Contributed by Michelle Kormos. Copyright © Kendall Hunt Publishing Company.

Day 13

FIGURE 13-1: Contributed by Tiffani Matlock. Copyright © Kendall Hunt Publishing Company.
FIGURE 13-2: Contributed by Kendall Blanton. Copyright © Kendall Hunt Publishing Company.
FIGURE 13-3: Contributed by Laynie Pruitt. Copyright © Kendall Hunt Publishing Company.
FIGURE 13-4: Contributed by Tonya Drew. Copyright © Kendall Hunt Publishing Company.
FIGURE 13-5: Contributed by Valerie McKay. Copyright © Kendall Hunt Publishing Company.
FIGURE 13-6: Contributed by Mahogany Turner. Copyright © Kendall Hunt Publishing Company.
FIGURE 13-7: Contributed by Becca Grecko. Copyright © Kendall Hunt Publishing Company.
FIGURE 13-8: Contributed by Rylee Foster. Copyright © Kendall Hunt Publishing Company.
FIGURE 13-9: Contributed by Maria G. Martinez. Copyright © Kendall Hunt Publishing Company.
FIGURE 13-10: Contributed by Caitlin Fowler. Copyright © Kendall Hunt Publishing Company.
FIGURE 13-11: Contributed by Christopher William Curtin. Copyright © Kendall Hunt Publishing Company.

Day 14

FIGURE 14-1: Courtesy of Jeanette Wachtman
FIGURE 14-2: Contributed by Rhianna Carter. Copyright © Kendall Hunt Publishing Company.
FIGURE 14-3: Contributed by Caleb Lopes. Copyright © Kendall Hunt Publishing Company.
FIGURE 14-4: Contributed by Lily Elizabeth Houston. Copyright © Kendall Hunt Publishing Company.

Day 16

FIGURES 16-1, 16-2, 16-3, 16-4, 16-5, 16-6, & 16-7: Contributed by Anthony Scali. Copyright © Kendall Hunt Publishing Company.
FIGURE 16-8: Contributed by Aaron Pappadouplos. Copyright © Kendall Hunt Publishing Company.

Day 18

FIGURE 18-1: DUCK, BEAR, AND BIRDHOUSE: Contributed by Sydni Hardeman. Copyright © Kendall Hunt Publishing Company.
FIGURE 18-2: Contributed by Salina Desai. Copyright © Kendall Hunt Publishing Company.
FIGURE 18-3: Contributed by Joseph Kirkland. Copyright © Kendall Hunt Publishing Company.
FIGURE 18-4: Contributed by Katheryn Perez. Copyright © Kendall Hunt Publishing Company.
FIGURE 18-5: Contributed by Laurie Davis. Copyright © Kendall Hunt Publishing Company.
FIGURE 18-6: Contributed by Carter Gramlins. Copyright © Kendall Hunt Publishing Company.
FIGURE 18-7: Contributed by Natalia Torres. Copyright © Kendall Hunt Publishing Company.
FIGURE 18-8: Contributed by Grace C. Dehner. Copyright © Kendall Hunt Publishing Company.
FIGURE 18-9: Contributed by Braeden Turner. Copyright © Kendall Hunt Publishing Company.
FIGURE 18-10: Contributed by Caitlin Faillet. Copyright © Kendall Hunt Publishing Company.
FIGURE 18-11: Contributed by Braeden Turner. Copyright © Kendall Hunt Publishing Company.

Day 19

TREE DRAWING: Courtesy of Jeanette Wachtman

Day 20

FIGURE 20-1: Courtesy of Jeanette Wachtman
LANDSCAPE (FARM) AND BUTTERFLY IMAGES: Courtesy of Jeanette Wachtman
ASK DEAR SHARLENE NEWSLETTER AND ARTWORK: Courtesy of Jeanette Wachtman

Introduction to Art Gallery

CAVE ARTIST PAINTING BY AUTHOR: Courtesy of Jeanette Wachtman

Art Gallery

FIGURE 21-1: Contributed by Morgan Ryan. Copyright © Kendall Hunt Publishing Company.
FIGURE 21-2: Contributed by Courtney Kilburn. Copyright © Kendall Hunt Publishing Company.
FIGURE 21-3: Contributed by Emily Campbell. Copyright © Kendall Hunt Publishing Company.
FIGURE 21-4: Contributed by Jessica Cervenizzo. Copyright © Kendall Hunt Publishing Company.
FIGURE 21-5: Contributed by Ashtyn Barber. Copyright © Kendall Hunt Publishing Company.
FIGURE 21-6: Contributed by Starr Taylor. Copyright © Kendall Hunt Publishing Company.
FIGURE 21-7: Contributed by Amanda Henderson. Copyright © Kendall Hunt Publishing Company.
FIGURE 9-2 & FIGURE 21-8: Contributed by Kevin Pham. Copyright © Kendall Hunt Publishing Company.
FIGURE 21-9: Contributed by Teran Wilson. Copyright © Kendall Hunt Publishing Company.
FIGURE 21-10: Contributed by Brittany Mauldin. Copyright © Kendall Hunt Publishing Company.
FIGURE 21-11: Contributed by Kala Howard. Copyright © Kendall Hunt Publishing Company.
FIGURE 21-12: Contributed by Ashley Shannon. Copyright © Kendall Hunt Publishing Company.
FIGURE 21-13: Contributed by Gabrielle Williams. Copyright © Kendall Hunt Publishing Company.
FIGURE 21-14: Contributed by Megan Brickhouse. Copyright © Kendall Hunt Publishing Company.
FIGURE 21-15: Contributed by Dawn Flowers. Copyright © Kendall Hunt Publishing Company.
FIGURE 21-16: Contributed by Sara Dobbins. Copyright © Kendall Hunt Publishing Company.
FIGURE 21-17: Contributed by Hannah Weldy. Copyright © Kendall Hunt Publishing Company.
FIGURE 21-18: Contributed by Elizabeth George. Copyright © Kendall Hunt Publishing Company.
FIGURE 21-19: Contributed by Audrey Howell. Copyright © Kendall Hunt Publishing Company.
FIGURE 21-20: Contributed by Amba Moss. Copyright © Kendall Hunt Publishing Company.
FIGURE 21-21: Contributed by Allison Dinkler. Copyright © Kendall Hunt Publishing Company.
FIGURE 21-22: Contributed by Hayley Whitaker. Copyright © Kendall Hunt Publishing Company.
FIGURE 21-23: Contributed by Danielle Newman. Copyright © Kendall Hunt Publishing Company.
FIGURE 21-24: Contributed by Rebecca Lindsey. Copyright © Kendall Hunt Publishing Company.
FIGURE 21-25: Contributed by Callison Payne. Copyright © Kendall Hunt Publishing Company.
FIGURE 21-26: Contributed by Brittany Miller. Copyright © Kendall Hunt Publishing Company.
FIGURE 21-27: Contributed by Michelle Zaino. Copyright © Kendall Hunt Publishing Company.

FIGURE 21-28: Contributed by Meagan Carey. Copyright © Kendall Hunt Publishing Company.

FIGURE 21-29: Contributed by Jessica Mullins. Copyright © Kendall Hunt Publishing Company.

FIGURE 21-30: Contributed by Amanda Folds. Copyright © Kendall Hunt Publishing Company.

FIGURE 21-31: Contributed by Kunyang Gou. Copyright © Kendall Hunt Publishing Company.

FIGURE 21-32: Contributed by Jessica Webb. Copyright © Kendall Hunt Publishing Company.

FIGURE 21-33: Contributed by Lauren Bell. Copyright © Kendall Hunt Publishing Company.

FIGURE 21-34: Contributed by Elizabeth Roth. Copyright © Kendall Hunt Publishing Company.

FIGURE 21-35: Courtesy of Jeanette Wachtman.

FIGURE 21-36 Contributed by Christa Jones. Copyright © Kendall Hunt Publishing Company.

FIGURE 21-37 AND FIGURE 21-54: Contributed by Adriana Thompson. Copyright © Kendall Hunt Publishing Company.

FIGURE 21-38: Contributed by Quint Allen. Copyright © Kendall Hunt Publishing Company.

FIGURE 21-39: Contributed by Marlo Williams. Copyright © Kendall Hunt Publishing Company.

FIGURE 21-40: Contributed by Bradley Johnson. Copyright © Kendall Hunt Publishing Company.

FIGURE 21-41: Contributed by Chloe Watts. Copyright © Kendall Hunt Publishing Company.

FIGURE 21-42: Contributed by Lea McDonald. Copyright © Kendall Hunt Publishing Company.

FIGURE 21-43: Contributed by Lauren Simerly. Copyright © Kendall Hunt Publishing Company.

FIGURE 21-44: Contributed by Natalie Wood. Copyright © Kendall Hunt Publishing Company.

FIGURE 21-45: Contributed by Macy West. Copyright © Kendall Hunt Publishing Company.

FIGURE 21-46: Contributed by Christi Lee. Copyright © Kendall Hunt Publishing Company.

FIGURE 21-47: Contributed by Caprice Mays. Copyright © Kendall Hunt Publishing Company.

FIGURE 21-48: Contributed by Alexis Champion. Copyright © Kendall Hunt Publishing Company.

FIGURE 21-49: Contributed by Eleanor Durrance. Copyright © Kendall Hunt Publishing Company.

FIGURE 21-50: Contributed by Elizabeth Wheeler. Copyright © Kendall Hunt Publishing Company.

FIGURE 21-51: Contributed by Joseph Kirkland. Copyright © Kendall Hunt Publishing Company.

FIGURE 21-52: Contributed by Jasmine Varela. Copyright © Kendall Hunt Publishing Company.

FIGURE 21-53: Contributed by Jamie Bunn. Copyright © Kendall Hunt Publishing Company.

END OF CHAPTER ART: Courtesy of Jeanette Wachtman

CPSIA information can be obtained
at www.ICGtesting.com
Printed in the USA
LVOW02s0829201216
518035LV00002B/2/P